Solomons Island and Vicinity

An Illustrated History

and Walking Tour

Compiled by Richard J. Dodds

Calvert Marine Museum

Solomons, Maryland

1995

Preface

In recent years Solomons Island and the surrounding area have become a mecca for visiting yachtsmen, tourists, and new residents, attracted by water, recreational amenities, and the rolling countryside dotted with tobacco barns and corn fields. The growth in the region has brought increased pressure for development which is changing both the physical landscape and traditional economic and social patterns. For twenty-five years the Calvert Marine Museum has tried to preserve and record this heritage through exhibits and publications.

For the tens of thousands of visitors who come to Solomons and the museum each year, there has been a need for a booklet to serve as a guide to the area. It is hoped that this publication will help document and encourage further interest in a unique part of historic Calvert County in Southern Maryland.

C. Douglass Alves Jr.
Director, Calvert Marine Museum

The rows of attractive dwellings, and houses being constructed, the neatly kept premises, the commodious and well managed hotel, the large and well stocked stores of general merchandise, the rush of business at the marine railways are indicative of considerable financial outlay and mark the industrial activity of Solomons. The visitor to the island town, connected by a substantial bridge to the mainland, might ask, what's the basis for all this activity and movement in trade? The answer would quickly be forthcoming, that it is all about under the water — the oyster.

"Solomons A Business Place," *Calvert Journal*, June 25, 1905

ACKNOWLEDGMENTS

With this publication the Calvert Marine Museum has brought together the talent and energies of a number of people. Much of the original research was done in the early 1980s by Dr. Ralph E. Eshelman and the late Clara M. Dixon. The product was a small booklet entitled *Historical Tours Through Southern Maryland – Solomons by Foot, Bicycle and Boat*, published in 1983 by the Southern Maryland Regional Library Association. This pioneering effort helped to record much of the history of the area that might otherwise have been lost.

Since that date, a large amount of new information has come to light through oral history, research into the land records, and by delving into old newspaper accounts. Compiling this material and making it readable would not have been possible without the help of dedicated staff and volunteers at the Calvert Marine Museum. CMM librarian, Paul Berry, was of invaluable help in sharing his knowledge of local land records and family histories, gathered from years of research. He also provided considerable editorial guidance. Robert Hurry and Rhoda Switzer offered many constructive comments and suggestions for the text in addition to locating sources of information in the museum's archival and photographic collections. Karen Stone lent freely of her computer skills and asked the tough questions when reviewing the drafts. Kit Kearney, with infinite patience and skill, entered the many changes that were made to the draft as new information came to light. And long–time museum supporter, Solomons resident, and recorder of local history — James LeRoy "Pepper" Langley — kindly reviewed the many drafts and pointed out a number of errors and omissions.

Other members of the community who were contacted and who provided invaluable assistance were: James Dodson, Daniel Dowell, Pauline Elliott, Charles Elliott, Doris Woodburn Johnson, Elizabeth Marsh Kriel, Linwood "Reds" Langley, Jon Shaw Lore, Althea Bowen McKenny, Jack Northam, Dorothy Ordwein, Janice Tierno, Martha Tongue, Thomas Tongue, and Virginia B. Lore von Zelinski.

This publication was made possible through the financial support of the MARPAT Foundation, Inc. of Washington, D.C. The MARPAT Foundation has generously supported the Calvert Marine Museum over the years in its goal to preserve and interpret the maritime heritage of Southern Maryland.

Lastly, it should be noted that the Calvert Marine Museum is solely responsible for the accuracy of the contents. Any accounts or other information that could correct or add to the historical record as presented within these pages would be most welcome.

The Narrows in 1936 with, right to left, the J.C. Lore & Sons Oyster House, H.M. Woodburn & Son Oyster House, and the United Methodist Church. In the foreground are charter boats of the Solomons sport fishing fleet (courtesy, Martin Luther King Public Library, Washington, D.C.).

INTRODUCTION

Solomons Island is located at the southern tip of Calvert County, in Southern Maryland, where the Patuxent River meets the Chesapeake Bay. For most of its history this sandy and low-lying island, comprising approximately thirty-seven acres, played little part in the significant historic events that shaped the tidewater area in the seventeenth, eighteenth, and early nineteenth centuries. Tobacco farming brought the first settlements and towns and associated commerce to the Patuxent region, but this occurred largely upriver. And, except for the burning of Point Patience in 1780, the American Revolution was chiefly fought to the south of Solomons — in tidewater Virginia. The War of 1812 came much closer as farms and settlements along the Patuxent River became targets for marauding British forces. Solomons, or Somervell's Island, as it was then known, bore mute witness to the passage of the British fleet up the Patuxent River on its way to burn Washington, and the unsuccessful attempt by a smaller American fleet, under Commodore Joshua Barney, to thwart their design. Even the Civil War of 1861–1865, when Marylanders often fought Marylanders, had no impact on this virtually uninhabited point of land.

It was not until the economic boom following the Civil War that Solomons came into prominence. Since the colonial period, the nearby harbor off Drum Point had provided a sheltered anchorage for sailing vessels bound up or down the Chesapeake. With the surge in the oyster industry after the Civil War, which made Maryland the world's leading supplier of the tasty bivalve, it was inevitable that someone would discover the island's potential as a center for oyster processing and the construction and repair of oystering vessels.

Such an individual was Isaac Solomon, a Baltimore businessman who, by 1868, had established a cannery together with associated wharf, lime kilns, marine railway, and workers' housing. Official recognition was given the community in 1870 when the United States Postal Service opened a post office.

Although Isaac Solomon's business was not successful (he sold it around 1875) the stage had been set. Benefiting from its accessible position at the mouth of the Patuxent River and the deep-water, sheltered anchorage at Drum Point, the town of Solomons quickly built a reputation as a center of shipbuilding and repairing, seafood harvesting, and the provisioning of sailing vessels engaged in the oystering business. In a land of scattered villages and farms, Solomons became Calvert County's most important commercial center.

Solomons was described in the issue of the weekly *Calvert Gazette* newspaper of November 12, 1892:

> There are about one hundred houses upon the island, including some stores which do an active business in the oyster season, and three shipyards . . . It is chiefly occupied by oystermen and fishermen.

In the same year, Dr. William H. Marsh, a local resident, observed that at night or in stormy weather the harbor would be crowded with hundreds of oyster boats and "on Sunday it is no unusual sight to see 300 or 400 vessels lying at anchor in the harbor."

It should be made clear at this point that Solomons, by the 1890s, was made up of two distinct communities — Solomons Island proper and Avondale on the mainland. Separating the two was a shallow stretch of water, approximately 550 feet wide, spanned by a somewhat rickety bridge. Most of the business activities were centered on the island itself; Avondale or Johnstown, as it was also called, was mainly residential. The inhabitants of Solomons at this time numbered around four hundred.

Like other tidewater communities of the late nineteenth and early twentieth centuries, Solomons was isolated, close–knit, and self–sufficient. Roads were few and became impassable in bad weather. The state provided a road from Solomons to Prince Frederick by 1915, and the Solomons portion, up to the bridge, was paved with crushed oyster shells. Beyond that it was a dirt road. An earlier dirt road was crossed by numerous gates that had to be opened and shut. Horse and ox–drawn wagons were the chief means of transport by land. As the *Calvert Journal* of February 13, 1897, lamented: "There is not in this whole section [Calvert County] a single railroad, a telegraph or telephone or a public conveyance of any kind." Solomons' link with the outside world was the twice–weekly steamboat from Baltimore, and its arrival was always a source of entertainment and great activity. Wagons met the steamboat at the wharf and delivered all manner of supplies and provisions to the local stores. Particularly welcome was ice, which was sold to the ice cream parlors before the town built its own ice plant. The steamer also provided a comfortable means to make occasional visits to Baltimore to shop or visit friends and relations. Every family also had its own boat which was used as people use the automobile today — to visit the store, go on a Sunday outing, or socialize with friends and neighbors along the creeks.

Residents of Solomons had to provide their own entertainment. In the heat of summer, older people and young children would often sit under the cool shade of the linden trees that stood near the town well. Older boys could often be found swimming near the bridge that crossed to the mainland or at the nearby flour mill. Sailing parties among the adults were quite popular. In wintertime, the men often gathered around the stove at Webster's store and exchanged the latest waterfront gossip. When the creeks and river froze, people of all ages went skating, some even made ice boats.

More organized activities included local chapters of fraternal clubs: Masons, Odd Fellows, Knights of Pythias, and Woodsmen of the World. And, for the mechanically inclined, there was the Patriotic Council No. 121, Junior Order, United American Mechanics. Solomons also took pride in a baseball team that played other communities in St. Mary's and Calvert Counties, as well as teams from Washington and Baltimore. The Solomons team also played against the crews of visiting naval vessels at their field at Sandy Point, on the extreme southern end of the island. Local talent also found an outlet in home-produced plays and theatricals and, occasionally, outside performers and lecturers came to town. In the summer months Chautauquas came for a week or two giving lectures on current news and history. The most anticipated entertainment, however, was the arrival of the James Adams Floating Theatre, a floating barge towed by two tugs. The Floating Theatre carried a drama troupe and orchestra which performed matinees and evenings, usually for a week's stand. Later renamed The Original Floating Theater, it visited Solomons every year, except one, between 1919 and 1939.

Making a living from the water required physical stamina and skill. The work was very seasonal and subject to the vagaries of nature. Second jobs were often a necessity. At an early age boys were expected to find work after school, such as feeding and watering the horses of visiting salesmen. Joseph C. Lore Jr. recalled collecting muskrat meat from a local trapper as a young boy, then rowing from boat to boat anchored at Drum Point and selling the meat at two for a quarter. For local African Americans, a number of whom were former slaves, life was usually harder. Only a few professions were open to them, as racial prejudice was prevalent here as elsewhere. Most lived in communities at the head of Mill Creek and on the Dowell peninsula.

With the arrival of the first automobile on Solomons around 1910, a way of life was irrevocably altered. It was a novel sight at the time. In 1983, former resident Ethelbert Lovett recalled, "when word came down that the first automobile was on its way to Solomons, Miss Susie Magruder, the principal of our three-room school, dismissed us for this historic occasion. Workmen in the shipyard dropped their tools and gathered around the new vehicle."

With the automobile came improved roads and new bridges, together with two other marvels of the age — the telephone as early as 1899 and electricity in 1928.

Solomons in the twentieth century gradually lost its isolation, a process that culminated in the construction of the Gov. Thomas Johnson Bridge in 1977, linking Calvert and St. Mary's Counties.

Changing economic patterns in the twentieth century also had a lasting impact on Solomons. The first decade of the twentieth century was a time of prosperity and growth. Solomons acquired a bank, a flour mill was constructed, and it had its own ice house and several fine boarding houses. Many of the community's largest homes were built at this time, particularly in the Johnstown/Avondale area. But by the late 1920s the region's economy was on a downswing. Declining oyster and fish harvests forced increasing numbers of watermen to look elsewhere to make a living. With the resulting decrease in the demand for workboats, local boatyards went out of business, or like M.M. Davis and Son, turned to building other types of craft, such as custom yachts. On the other hand, Solomons witnessed a steady growth in the business of providing recreation to "outsiders" — starting with summer boarding houses and charter fishing boats in the early years of this century.

The general decline of the seafood industry and the slump in boatbuilding and related trades were magnified by the Great Depression of the 1930s. And, to aggravate matters, the greatest natural disaster to hit Solomons occurred during this time — the August 23, 1933, storm. The lower end of the island was submerged, oyster beds and packing houses were damaged, the steamboat wharf was torn away and destroyed, and many boats were demolished, damaged, or lost. But for Solomons, the lean times were tempered somewhat by the income provided by sports fishermen who frequented the area. However, it was America's entry into World War II which brought new wealth to Solomons and the surrounding communities. This development permanently altered the old way of life.

In 1942–1943 three navy bases were established at the mouth of the Patuxent River, transforming the landscape and economy: the Naval Amphibious Training Base on the Dowell peninsula; the Naval Mine Warfare Test Station at Point Patience (known locally as the Ordnance Lab); and the Patuxent Naval Air Station across the river in St. Mary's County. These three facilities made a major contribution to the war effort and, although only the third is in existence today, they brought new, often better-paying jobs to local residents, and flushed the area with "strangers." Between 1942 and 1945 the population of Solomons increased from 263 to more than 2,600, taxing the area's resources to the utmost. But it was the local watermen who had the hardest time as the traditional oystering and crabbing grounds were disrupted by all the military activity.

Postwar population growth and development, changing economic patterns, and improved communication and transportation brought an end to the isolated and self-sufficient community that was Solomons. Restaurants and gift shops have replaced the general stores and grocery stores of former years. Wooden boatbuilding has long since disappeared and, more recently, so too have the commercial fisheries. But Solomons' focus still lies with the waters nearby, in the shape of its marinas and marine suppliers, charter boat operators, pilot's station, Chesapeake Biological Laboratory, and the Calvert Marine Museum.

With this publication, the Calvert Marine Museum hopes to document and preserve a little of what Solomons used to be: the churches, businesses, schools, homes, and people that formed the heart of the community. It is very much a walk through history.

For clarity, the book has been divided into three sections: Solomons Island proper; Avondale/Johnstown; and the surrounding area. It is not intended to be all-inclusive, and represents the best information available at the time. The museum would welcome any corrections to the facts as they are presented.

Solomons Island Historical Sketch

The present–day Solomons covers an area that includes the earlier Solomons Island, a late–nineteenth century "development" given the name of Avondale, and additional land to the north that was originally farms. The island itself was variously known as Bourne's Island (about 1680), Somervell's Island (1740–1814), and Sandy Island (1827–1865). The land was most likely part of the early land grant of Eltonhead Manor that included much of the southern part of Calvert County in the seventeenth and eighteenth centuries, but the manor was divided and sold as separate tracts as the years progressed. Chancery records of Maryland dated June 1827 show that a Nathaniel Baker, then deceased, bought from Dr. William Somervell, also then deceased, "an island in the Patuxent River, at or near its mouth." Mr. Baker is then said to have sold it to Bennett Sollers, who in turn sold it to James Tongue, who conveyed it to George Bourne. Land records of the first half of the nineteenth century are difficult to trace because of the courthouse fire of 1882 that destroyed all land records prior to that date.

Mr. Bourne's deed to the island resulted from a court case in which he was declared to be the owner. By 1853 the island was owned by a Littleton Johnson, of whom nothing is known, and he in turn sold it that year to a William Buckler, also unidentified, who in August 1856 sold the island to a group of Baltimore investors who were buying sizable tracts of land at the mouth of the Patuxent River in both Calvert and St. Mary's Counties for reasons not specified. These land purchases were in the name of Richard B. Fitzgerald who was a partner in the Baltimore firm of Fitzgerald and Booth, commission merchants, but the funds were one–half from Fitzgerald and Booth and one–half from the Peruvian importer Frederick L. Barreda, then living in New York.

After the illness of Richard B. Fitzgerald in 1864, the circuit court of Baltimore appointed a committee to handle his affairs, with one of the first transactions being the sale in 1865 of a tract of eighty acres called "Sandy Island" to Isaac Solomon. He immediately began to develop the island and by at least 1868 was advertising his canning establishment at "Solomon's Island." This was the first large–scale canning factory on the Patuxent River.

The late W. E. Northam, long–time Solomons Island resident, described this plant from memory in 1954. It was a single–story building about four hundred feet long paralleling what is today the state road. A "T" extended out over the water. The center section was two stories high; the office was located here. The office was square, with a cupola and flag staff on top. This description is very similar to an early etching of the proposed development for the island shown in this booklet. The original location of this building is uncertain, but it apparently was destroyed by neglect and numerous tropical storms that hit the Maryland Tidewater in the 1880s. Heavy winds in March 1890 finally destroyed the remaining part.

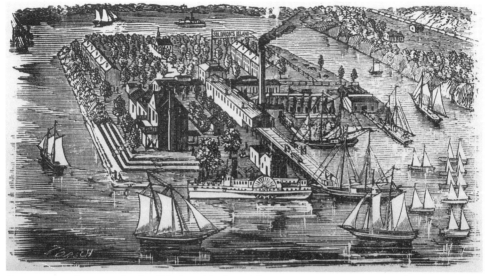

A contemporary but somewhat fanciful view of the Isaac Solomon Oyster Canning Company from an unknown source. The T-shaped main building is clearly visible as are the lime kilns on the right, still evident on an 1893 plat of Solomons Island. The Solomons House is probably the building on the far left.

One writer remarked, "This cove oyster house was away ahead of its time. The operating system was original. [Solomon] owned all vessels supplying oysters for the house, and the captains and the crews were paid by the month. The by–product shells were burned, and the farmers had low–priced lime close at hand. All surplus shells were used in low places, with the result that today some of the most valuable parts of the island was once crabbing water." (*Calvert Independent* Tri–Centenary Edition, September 23, 1954.)

Isaac Solomon (1819–1895) had established a canning factory in Baltimore by 1860; in 1861, he was credited with the first application to commercial canning of an earlier discovery of adding calcium chloride to water in order to increase the boiling temperature from 212 degrees Fahrenheit to 240 degrees Fahrenheit or higher. This reduced the processing time for canning from four or five hours to only thirty or forty minutes.

Isaac Solomon's purchase of "Sandy Island" allowed him to expand his canning operation and locate closer to the oyster grounds. He leased small lots on the island to many persons who paid a yearly rent varying from $9 to $21. A plat of lots by number was made by Thomas L. Grover in 1870. In the same year the first bridge, a footbridge 550 feet long, connected the island with the mainland. There was even an association known as the Alpha Building Association of Solomons which may have come into existence as an agency from which persons could borrow money to build homes on land they had purchased.

As early as 1868 a railroad from Baltimore to Drum Point was contemplated to take advantage of the excellent harbor between Drum Point and Solomons Island, considered by some to be one of the finest harbors on the East Coast. By the 1870s, the railway right-of-way had been surveyed, but financial difficulties brought a halt to any construction. Revived interest in the 1880s and 1890s resulted in construction of the roadbed, but no tracks had been laid when more financial difficulties brought the project to a halt.

By 1880 the census listed fifty-one different households and 237 residents. Local tradition holds that the Solomons fishing fleet exceeded five hundred vessels, many locally built.

Isaac Solomon's enterprise collapsed in the mid-1870s, in large part due to the failure of the proposed railroad from Baltimore to Drum Point, and he lost the island to Baltimore creditors. In 1879, most of Solomons Island and the cannery were bought by John S. Farren and Thomas R. Moore for $6,225. Mr. Farren was owner of the New Haven, Connecticut, J. S. Farren Company which opened an oyster canning house in Baltimore and decided to buy the Solomons holding as a branch facility. Capt. Thomas Moore, owner of the largest private fleet of vessels in Maryland, was looking for a suitable harbor where he could establish a repair and maintenance facility for his nearly two hundred vessels. Captain Moore sold his interest in the island at auction in 1892 for $10,000 to Burdette H. Farren, brother of John, and their two sisters. The Farrens immediately invested more money into the island when in 1893 a new, two-story warehouse was built near the steamboat wharf and a 1,323-foot-long bulkhead was constructed along the lower, eastern end of the island.

In the late nineteenth and early twentieth centuries the U. S. Government took an increasing interest in the Patuxent River as the location for a number of installations and activities.

In 1889 a floating hospital ship was moored near Solomons by the U. S. Marine Hospital Service, to cater to the medical needs of the crews aboard oyster dredge boats sheltering in the harbor. This was followed by the establishment in 1890 of a "third class relief station" in the town of Solomons itself.

Three years later, in 1893, the government inspected Hog Island, on the St. Mary's side of the river, with a view to building a quarantine station. Money was actually appropriated but the project failed when the landowner, Mr. P. H. Tuck, refused to sell.

The navy, too, was showing interest. Around 1904–1919 the training ship USS *Severn* (ex *Chesapeake*), a magnificent white-painted, full-rigged vessel, was frequently at Solomons. Local waters were also used by the infant naval Torpedo Boat Flotilla for special speed tests. They frequently employed the anchored *Severn* as a base for speed performance trials on the Barren Island speed course.

Beginning in 1898 the navy looked seriously at establishing a dry dock at Drum Point. Many local residents and state politicians were actively in favor of the idea, but the failure to extend a railway to Drum Point ultimately doomed this project as well. A $1,400,000 appropriation was initially included in the navy's 1907 appropriation bill, but it was later dropped.

In 1905, however, the navy selected the mouth of the Patuxent as the best site in the tidewater to test the famous *Dewey* floating dry dock, recently constructed at Sparrow's Point, Baltimore, and completed at Solomons by the Maryland Steel Company. This mammoth, 500 x 100-foot long, 16,000-ton vessel needed deep water for its test and the waters off Solomons fitted the bill. In the final test for the craft the armored cruiser USS *Colorado* was dry-docked, followed by the battleship USS *Iowa*. In both cases, the *Dewey* passed with flying colors. She was towed to the Philippines and arrived on July 10, 1906, after an adventuresome voyage.

SOLOMONS ISLAND TOUR

Perhaps the best place to begin a tour of Solomons is at the Calvert Marine Museum, located about one-half mile north of Solomons Island. Dedicated to man's interrelationship with his environment on the Patuxent River estuary, there are several exhibits dealing with Solomons shipbuilding, Patuxent River watermen, and early local history.

Once you've familiarized yourself with the region's history, you may either walk, bicycle, or cruise by water around historic Solomons Island and Solomons Harbor. A boat ride on the museum's historic oyster buyboat, *Wm. B. Tennison*, built in 1899, is an excellent way to see the region from the water during her season, May through October.

Listed below in numerical sequence are the sites and structures that correspond to the accompanying location maps. There is a map for each of the three areas: Solomons Island, the Avondale/Johnstown community, and the surrounding district.

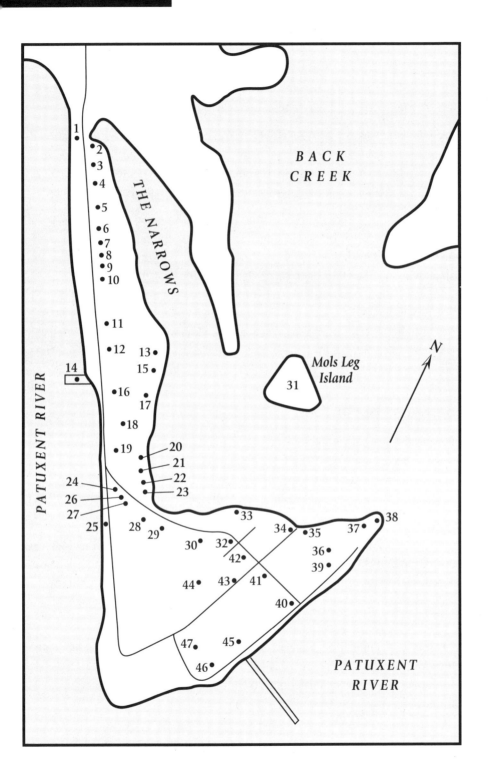

1. THE BRIDGE/TIDE BOX

The present-day link between Solomons Island and the mainland is a small bridge or "tidebox," hardly noticeable to motorists. But throughout the nineteenth century the island and mainland were separated by over 550 feet of shallow water that was not bridged until 1870. The narrow neck of water running up the east side of the island to the bridge was known appropriately as the Narrows. At its head, on the mainland (Johnstown) side was located a slaughter house (see #49), steam-driven flour mill, and ice house (see #50).

Shipbuilder James T. Marsh sawed the lumber and built the first wooden bridge. In 1893 much of the bridge was washed away in a tropical storm leaving the islanders to resort to boats for communication with the mainland until the bridge was repaired.

By 1905 the bridge was in a dilapidated condition and complaints were frequent. Heavy wagonloads were forced to cross the shallows, which could be somewhat hazardous. In 1907 the bridge was replaced with another structure of wood and concrete for which James Henry Marsh sawed the lumber.

The new causeway and seawall under construction in 1915, replacing the old wooden bridge to Solomons Island. In the background is the Methodist Church.

In 1915 the construction of a cement seawall on the island side enabled the main road to be widened and the gap between the island and mainland to be narrowed. The road at the northern end of the island, which previously was about ten feet lower than the adjacent buildings, was raised to the same level by bringing in large amounts of sand and gravel. For this job the Stabaugh Construction Company of Chicago used a large group of Russian laborers who were housed in the old flour mill. Local resident Joe Lore Jr. worked on this project as a water boy for sixty cents for a ten-hour day.

Further work in 1948-1949, 1957, and again in 1985 resulted in the wide but short tidebox we see today. The area between the tidebox and the Methodist Church (see #5) is mostly oyster shell fill from the two oyster houses located here.

2. J. C. Lore Oyster House (1888–1978)

Joseph C. Lore Sr. came to Solomons from New Jersey in 1888 as an oyster buyer for his brother's New Jersey (Delaware Bay) packing house. For a period of time in the early 1900s, Captain Lore also bought and sold soft crabs from a waterfront site near the old flour mill (see #50). He moved across the Narrows to build his own packing house here in 1922, a one-story building set on pilings. It was destroyed by the 1933 hurricane. The existing structure was built in 1934 and has been enlarged several times. During its operation J.C. Lore and Sons bought, processed, and sold finfish, crabs, and oysters. Fresh seafood was shipped by mail and truck to markets as far away as the Midwest. This company did some of the first oyster farming, leased its own oyster beds in the Patuxent, and was noted for keeping meticulous records of oyster spat set, water conditions, and oyster growth. The company is said to have been the first to pack caviar on the Western Shore, which was shipped to Europe in the 1920s; it came from sturgeon caught in the Potomac River. During the summer months charterboat

Lore & Sons Oyster House in 1936. Standing in the foreground, left to right, are Melvin Jones, Joseph C. Lore Jr., G.I Rupert ("Dick") Lore, Joseph C. Lore Sr., and Frank Tongue.

fishing was also offered. When America entered World War II, the company won contracts to provide frozen seafood to the armed forces.

Joseph C. Lore Sr. died in 1945 and the business was carried on by J. C. Lore Jr. and G. I. Rupert Lore. In 1961 the partnership between the two brothers was dissolved and the following year Alton S. Kersey, J. C. Lore Jr.'s son-in-law, became active in the management of the oyster house.

The Lore company operated several boats including the 47-foot Hooper Island launch *Penguin*, now in the Calvert Marine Museum's collection, the charter boat *Loree*, and the 60-foot oyster boat *Wm. B. Tennison*, the museum's historic cruise boat. Associated with the business, but owned by William Preston Lore, was the 55-foot converted bugeye *Sidney R. Riggin*. The Calvert Marine Museum acquired the packing plant in 1979. It now houses a commercial fisheries exhibit, "Seasons of Abundance, Seasons of Want: Making a Living from the Waters of the Patuxent," and "Built to Work," an exhibit portraying traditional boatbuilding methods. The building was placed on the National Register of Historic Places in 1983.

3. FIRST CALVERT MARINE MUSEUM (SITE)

This property was leased by the late John Bluster to the Calvert County Historical Society for use as the Calvert Marine Museum from 1969 until 1975 for $1 per year. The structure, later used as part of the adjacent restaurant, was built completely by volunteer labor with donated materials and funds. The museum opened here on October 18, 1970. It outgrew these facilities and moved in 1975 to its present site at the old Solomons School (see #68). The original museum building was destroyed by fire in 1985.

4. H.M. WOODBURN & SON/WOODBURN RESTAURANT/PIER ONE RESTAURANT (SITE)

The Woodburn Oyster House was established on this site in 1918 by Harry M. Woodburn. Mr. Woodburn came to Solomons from St. Mary's County around 1885 and oystered and crabbed before opening the packing house. Built on stilts out over the waters of the Narrows, many of the oyster shells shucked at this facility now serve as the fill around it. Woodburn also had a crab shedding business next door to the oyster house. Preston Woodburn and his wife Violet opened a restaurant in the third oyster house built on this site in the early 1940s. It later became the Pier 1 Restaurant which burned in 1985. Another restaurant now occupies the site.

From 1943 until 1945, Henry Gasque operated a bus service between Washington, D.C., and Solomons Island. Known as the Express Bus Line, Woodburn's Restaurant was the bus terminus until it was moved to Bowen's Inn in 1945.

Adjoining the oyster house on the right, the present bait and tackle shop was opened as a grocery in 1927. A screened–in porch served as an ice cream parlor. The same year Harry A. Woodburn, son of H. M. Woodburn, started a fishing party business. At the time, a sports fisherman could charter a boat for four hours for $20. Each charter boat was named after a grandchild of H. M. Woodburn.

Capt. Harry Woodburn piloted the new fishing cruiser *Leroy* to the first Chesapeake Bay

H.M. Woodburn & Son Oyster House around 1927.

Fishing Fair, held at Tilghman in 1936. The *Leroy* was the center of attraction for the fishing guides and watermen. This inspired other fishing captains to build similar charter boats which soon were used up and down the Bay. Prior to this, skiffs and other workboats were used with no conveniences specific to the sports fisherman.

Today, a tackle shop and charter boat fishing center still occupy the site, although it has been leased by the family since 1989. It is the longest continuously operated charter boat business in Solomons.

5. Solomons United Methodist Church

The United Methodist Church was built in 1870 by James T. Marsh and was the first church on the island. Land for the church was donated by Isaac Solomon. Prior to its construction, Richard Norwood, a merchant who arrived in 1866, held services in private homes and in the "canning shop" (see #41).

Around 1899 the church was remodeled by lowering the pitch of the roof, changing the front, and ceiling the interior. Further changes in 1911 included a new front addition.

When built, the church was on the most northerly land on Solomons Island and in an exposed position. Erosion of the adjoining graveyard was a recurring problem and most of the cemetery was later moved off the island. One of the few graves to remain is that of Capt. Thomas Oliver, who died in 1927, and is one of the few known Civil War veterans of Solomons.

Approaches to Solomons Island in 1906. For many years the Methodist Church was the northernmost building on the island.

6. Langley Lunch Room/Adams Ferry/Langley Ferry (site)

In 1931, Joseph Rodie Langley and sons started an all-night restaurant here, commonly known as Langley Lunch Room. On most Saturday nights a string orchestra from St. Mary's County entertained here. Motor and row boats were for hire, with fishing party boats available day or night. Clients included well-known personalities such as Gene Autry.

From 1934 to 1939, John Quincy Adams of Colonial Beach, Va., operated the ferry *Miss Constance* from here. The 60-foot ferry was built to accommodate both passengers and vehicles and ran across the Patuxent to St. Mary's County. James "Reds" Forrest was the captain and Stanley Adams the engineer. This service replaced an earlier ferry run by Captain Swift (see # 35). Mr. Adams also supplied provisions to the Standard Oil Fleet (see #93) mothballed in the river.

From 1941 until 1977, Capt. Leon Langley provided a commuter ferry service between Solomons and the Patuxent River Naval Air Station on the 48-foot *Miss Solomons*. Even after the Patuxent River Bridge at Benedict was opened in 1951, she still saved passengers a sixty-mile commute by car.

About a dozen of the commuters had second cars, ten- to twenty-years old, and bought secondhand for as little as $100 to $150. Kept on the Naval Station, license plates weren't even required. The cars were shared by other commuters who paid $1 per week for the ride. For the first year, there was no dock at the Naval Station and Langley had to row the commuters ashore.

For a time, a slot machine was installed on board the *Miss Solomons*. It is claimed that the longest continuing poker game ever, was played by the commuters going to and from work on board this ferry. The completion of the Gov. Thomas Johnson Bridge (see #70) in December 1977 caused the end of the ferry service. The state paid the Langley family $7,000 for the loss of business. Langley Lunch Room was renamed Fisherman's Inn in 1957. It burned in 1987, along with Langley's residence which had been built in 1904. A new restaurant now occupies the site.

7. LOCUST INN

Named for the two big locust trees that once graced the front yard, this rooming house was established prior to 1911 by George Condiff Sr. and his wife Catherine. In that year, weekly rates were six dollars, and up to twenty guests could be accommodated. After their deaths, George Jr. and his sister, Marga-

Guests in front of the Locust Inn, early 1900s.

ret, managed the inn. It is still operating today under other management.

8. MISS SUSIE MAGRUDER'S SCHOOLHOUSE (SITE)

Thomas R. Moore sold this land to the Board of County School Commissioners in August 1882 for $200. Replacing the first school on Solomons (see #43), a new, larger, two–room school was built on this site sometime after 1882, although few particulars are known. In 1899 a new, three–room school was dedicated and this

The three-room schoolhouse and Files ice cream parlor sometime before 1912. Note the difference in height between the main road and the buildings.

served until 1925. Miss M. Susan Magruder was the principal and taught here for twenty–one years. A shed on the waterfront contained coal for the school's potbellied stove and students took turns filling the stove in the winter. In 1911 an artesian well was sunk to provide water for the students.

9. FILES ICE CREAM PARLOR AND KOPP BLACKSMITH SHOP (SITE)

William H. Files and his wife Edna made ice cream using a small gas–powered engine in a little building behind the Files family home which was purchased in 1906 from Capt. Jesse Bramble. Ice was brought in by steamer or bought from The Calvert Ice Company ice house (see #34). Prior to this, the Files had at least two other ice cream parlors in a different location.

Files's father William, a ship carpenter, had emigrated from Germany with his seven children and settled in Solomons. By 1896 William H. Files was described as a confectioner. Three years later, in 1899, the entrepreneurial Files was one of the first inhabitants to acquire a wind–up gramophone and offered to give six tunes for twenty–five cents to any number of persons.

In 1907 Files moved his house to the rear of the lot and a new store was erected in the front, from which he continued to sell ice cream and confectioneries. It was undoubtedly popular with students at the school next door. The ice cream parlor was also a favorite of the congregation of the nearby Methodist Church, most of whom would gather there after the Sunday night service.

Mrs. Edna Files married John Kopp after her first husband's death. Mr. Kopp opened a blacksmith shop on the water side of the property. Here he made oyster tongs and metal parts for boats. He also worked for the M. M. Davis Shipyard as a blacksmith. His father, William, had emigrated from Germany and was also a blacksmith.

10. O'BERRY ICE AND COAL COMPANY (SITE)/O'BERRY MARINE

Alexander O'Berry operated an ice and coal business on this spot from 1925 to 1935. Later, Sherman O'Berry opened a marine store which today is called O'Berry Marine. This building stands on the foundation of the former Files ice cream parlor (see #9).

11. CIGAR MANUFACTURER/BAKE SHOP/GARNER STORE (SITE)

A. M. Sewell established a cigar manufacturing business on this site before 1884. The Sewells lived on Farren Avenue near "The Maples" boarding house. Later, the site was a bakery and finally a grocery store, operated by George A. Garner from approximately 1906 to 1918. Garner moved the old Norwood Store (see #5) to this property in 1905, in front of his home. The building there today is thought to be this store, although it is now a residence. Many of the local men gathered here in the evenings to exchange news and tell stories.

12. ABELL'S INN

This house was made into a rooming house in 1931 by Mrs. Olivia Abell with six rooms upstairs. Her husband Thomas died in the flu epidemic of 1934 and by 1936 it was closed. During World War II, Leon and Clara Langley ran the business and added a dining room on the first floor. Several years after the war they sold the property. It is now a gift shop.

13. M. M. DAVIS SHIPYARD (SOLOMONS) (SITE)

Marcellus M. Davis established the M. M. Davis & Co. shipyard on Lot #6 along the Narrows of Solomons Island in 1885. In 1890, he developed an expanded boatbuilding operation on Lots #12 and #13 and built his residence along the river side of the property. There he established the M. M. Davis Marine Railway Company in 1892. Although the company declared bankruptcy in 1898 and Davis removed to Baltimore, he returned to Solomons in 1900 and resumed boatbuilding at the railway site. The shipyard built many well known schooners, bugeyes, and tugs. In 1910 Davis purchased property on Mill Creek and began developing an expanded shipyard (see #85). His yard on the island continued as a repair facility until about 1918.

Members of the Davis family in 1920. Marcellus M. Davis is at top right with his son Clarence below.

14. Evan's Pavilion/Solomons Pier

Evan's Pavilion was established in 1919 by Perry T. Evans along with his son Reynold, who got the idea from a pavilion at Nice, France, where he was stationed during World War I. Over the years the structure has been a dance hall (with orchestras on weekends from Washington), ice cream parlor, movie theater, and

Evan's Pavilion as originally built.

restaurant. In the early 1920s a waterslide was built from the top of the structure where small boats on wheels carried people into the waters of the Patuxent River. In 1934 an addition was made which later became a movie house. Movies cost fifteen cents. Each patron had to carry his own folding chair to the multipurpose room and a five-cent rebate was given if the chair was returned. In June 1941, the local newspapers brought excitement to the community with news of a new modern movie projector being installed. Movies were shown here up until the 1960s. There were nine rooms rented out from the late 1930s to the 1960s. It is now a restaurant known as Solomons Pier.

15. Evans' Bakery/Thomas Crab House (site)

Perry Evans's son Reynold opened a bakery behind the Evans's family home located on this site. It stayed in business for only a short time between 1926 and 1928 and has since been torn down. People came by boat from as far away as Olivet to buy bread. It was also delivered by truck to places like Broomes Island. After World War II, Thomas Crab House operated here behind the family home. Steamed crabs were sold to private customers as well as local restaurants. It is now a private residence.

16. St.Peter's Protestant Episcopal Church

Built in 1889, this is the only surviving board–and–batten, Gothic–style church in Calvert County. Before its construction, local parishioners had a six mile horse–and–buggy ride to Middleham Chapel. St. Peter's and the first Catholic church, St. Mary's Star of the Sea, (see #58) were designed by Dr. George Chambers, "a physi-

St. Peter's Episcopal Church with the Evans family home behind.

cian and architect." Appropriately in a community of watermen, it was named for the great fisherman, the Apostle St. Peter. Total cost, including land, bell, and furnishings, was about $1,800. The windows, which were originally of marbleized opaque glass, have gradually been replaced with memorial stained glass. During the tenure of Rev. Benjamin E. Lovett (1911–1913) the parish acquired a motorized log canoe named *George Leakin* which was often used when visiting parishioners.

17. U.S.O. (site)/Yacht Club

The United Services Organization was originally housed in a pavilion on the Chesapeake Biological Laboratory (see #45) pier beginning in May 1944. A new building, designed to serve the needs of the many service personnel in the area, was constructed in 1944 and first occupied in December of that year. A grand opening was held in May 1945. The Solomons Island Yacht Club raised funds for the building and in 1947 took possession of it as their headquarters, a role which continues today.

18. NORTHAM HOUSE (SITE)/BOWEN'S INN

Established in 1918 on the Northam family homesite by George Mortimer Bowen, a former oysterman, this inn became one of the favorite fishing headquarters for many congressional and sports figures out of Washington, D.C. Prominent among them was Sam Rayburn, longtime Speaker of the House of Representatives. The inn enjoyed a fine reputation for its good food, and played host to Arthur Godfrey, John F. Kennedy, Harry Truman, and many state governors and officials.

Edgar Bowen, Mortimer's son, ran waterfowl hunting trips from here on the Patuxent River and Chesapeake Bay. The "beer garden," or outside bar, was a first in Solomons. It was built in 1927 as an annex to the original inn, then converted in the 1930s. In 1937 a large three–story building was added immediately behind the old house. During World War II rooms were rented to accommodate the wives of naval personnel stationed in the area. In 1951 forty rooms were available, at a cost of three to four dollars a night. The business is still in operation as a restaurant and bar.

For several years beginning in World War II a bus service ran between Solomons and Washington, D.C., and between Solomons and Baltimore. After 1945 the driver spent the night at Bowen's and kept the bus there. Prior to this service, owner Thomas Parran started the West Shore Transit Company between Solomons and Annapolis. Here passengers connected with the electric train to Baltimore.

The original Bowen's Inn, formerly the Northam family home.

The old Northam House, the original inn, was a large Victorian mansard–roof house built about 1888 for Capt. James W. Northam who came to Solomons from Accomac County, Virginia. It was torn down about 1976.

19. Crockett Store/Bafford Store (site)

This building was the William Crockett Store from 1890 until 1909. When it opened in 1890, it made the seventh store on the island. Mr. Crockett made wooden shafts for hand oyster tongs and also sold small boats from his backyard. At Christmas each year, Mrs. Crockett, who operated a millinery from the store, decorated the front windows with toys and dolls. In 1909, Joseph J. Bafford purchased the store and attached dwelling from the Crocketts and moved his store from the intersection of Sollers Wharf Road and Route 2/4. Thomas Bafford and his wife Bertie maintained a grocery and dry goods store at this site until his retirement in 1947. He was known as a staunch Republican in this strongly Democratic community. The attached home was razed in 1977 but the store still stands.

20. De Boy Railway and Machine Shop (site)

Known as the Patuxent Garage and Machine Shop, this business operated from about 1927 until 1947 when Frank De Boy left his yard to work for the nearby boatyard started by his son-in-law, Rupert ("Dick") Lore. The belt-driven machinery in the De Boy shop was powered by a large gasoline engine. Previously, the Thomas Moore Shipyard occupied part of this site.

De Boy moved from Baltimore to Solomons in 1925. After DeBoy left, Eugene Lankford ran it as a machine shop up until the late 1950s. The garage burned down in 1984.

21. Solomon & Son & Davis/Alexander Somervell/Thomas Moore Shipyard (site)

The shipyard was originally the Solomon & Son & Davis Railway, established in 1871 by Isaac and Charles Solomon in partnership with Isaac Davis. The railway was purchased by Alexander Somervell, Charles Solomon's father-in-law, at a public auction in August 1875 and operated by him until 1879.

Thomas R. Moore, originally from Dorchester County, operated a shipyard at this site from 1880 to 1906. He is reputed to have owned the largest private, commercial fleet in Maryland (nearly two hundred vessels). Moore formed a partnership with John H. Farren of Connecticut and bought Solomons Island in 1879 for $6,225. Moore's yard did mainly repair and maintenance work, although by the 1890s and 1900s he leased space to other boat builders including Martin P. McDonagh and George T. Dawson. The latter joined with Baltimore interests to form the Dawson Shipbuilding Company, under whose name the yard was leased in 1906.

The Thomas Moore shipyard crowded with sailing vessels under construction or being repaired (courtesy, The Mariners' Museum, Newport News, VA).

Moore's son, Thomas W. Moore, purchased the cannery in 1905 on the farm of William H. Hellen on the Dowell peninsula (see #23). When the 3,000–square-foot cannery burned in October of the following year, the boiler was moved to a new factory at Town Creek in St. Mary's County. Moore and his son were also commission merchants in Baltimore.

22. Dorsey's Inn/Bradburn's Crab House (site)

Tom J. Dorsey ran fishing parties, rented boats, and sold sandwiches, beer, and soft drinks from this establishment. During World War II the business closed but it resumed for a few years after 1945. On the property once stood a large wooden pilothouse off an unknown steamship. It used to house Capt. Bennie Abell and the crew of the motorboat *Speedway*, which brought motor oil from Baltimore to the community for the Red Sea Oil Company. Tom Dorsey later used it as a home until the late 1930s. Next door was Bradburn's Crab House where the Bradburn family picked and sold crab meat from the 1950s until 1989. Capt. James B. Bradburn crabbed, oystered, and fished when not working at Patuxent Naval Air Station. His wife Oretha ran the crab house.

23. HAYWARD/JOHNSON STORE (SITE)

George W. Hayward, who came from the Eastern Shore, opened a general store at this site at least as early as 1884. By 1890, when an artesian well was sunk at the

Solomons harbor with the Hayward/Johnson store on the left and the De Boy marine railway and machine shop on the right.

store, the business was operated in partnership with George W. Johnson. Johnson also came from the Eastern Shore, originally to work as a clerk in the nearby Webster Store. After the death of Hayward in 1894, he became sole proprietor and sold dry goods, groceries, and hardware. Buggy whips were a particular specialty. By 1905, however, Johnson ran into financial difficulties and was forced to sell at auction the contents of the store, his sloop *Annie C. Johnson*, three bugeyes, and his canning factory on the Dowell peninsula, built in 1903 (see #21). Later that year Johnson reopened the store, although the property was still owned by the Hayward heirs. Later owners included Dick Parks and finally Asa C. Ketcham during the 1920s. By about 1929 this structure had been converted to a warehouse for J.C. Webster's store (see #29). Later still the site became a machine shop run by Jim Schultz.

24. POST OFFICE (SITE)

This was the site of the fourth post office. The first had been at Isaac Solomon's store near the steamboat wharf. The second was a small building across from the old Parish Hall (see #40). For a short period around 1898 the post office was located at the Webster Store (see #29). Isaac Solomon's son, Charles S. Solomon, was appointed the first postmaster in 1870. William Solomon took over in 1872, and he was replaced by John D. Shenton in 1875. For a short while in 1900 the post office moved to Olivet and T.P. (Pert) Evans was postmaster, but it was re–established at Solomons the same year. The post office built in 1900 was on land that was part of the Thomas Moore shipyard. The *Calvert Gazette* on November 2, 1907, reported that Evans was no longer using a rowboat to take the outgoing mail to the steam-boat wharf but was using a pushcart instead.

When the new state road was laid out in 1913, the post office was in the way. It was apparently moved a short distance, alongside the home of Walter Files. This post office was the first built expressly for use as a post office. For the first time mail-boxes could be rented.

The post office was enlarged and William H. Condiff became postmaster in 1914. At retirement in 1952, his brother George took over. When George W. Condiff Jr. retired in 1958, the post office moved to the building (demolished in 1995) just south of the J. C. Lore Oyster House that also served as a general store (see #2). In 1978 the post office was moved off the island to the Patuxent Plaza shopping center. The current residence on the site of the fourth post office was made in the 1960s by

Post office at the corner of Charles Street and Patuxent Avenue. Rekar's Hotel appears on the far left, before alterations.

joining it and the adjacent building together. The latter building was used by the United States Navy as a shore patrol headquarters during World War II. After the war it was a barbershop run by Clyde Dove.

25. DORSEY BOAT RENTAL (SITE)

Said to be the first on the island, Peter A. Dorsey operated this business. During the late 1930s rowboat rentals were $1 per day or $5 per week; motor boats were $5 for four hours with each person over five an additional $1.

26. ABBOTT'S BARBERSHOP/DOCTOR'S OFFICE (SITE)

A barbershop was operating on this site as early as 1893. During the late 1930s, when Mitchell ("Britches") Abbott owned the business, it was very popular and clientele included local residents, crew from the Standard Oil Fleet, and Eastern Shore watermen. His shop was the front room of his house. Abbot was a colorful character and was known for his red, white, and blue suspenders. Dr. Edward Quarrels and later Dr. Page Jett maintained a once-a-week patient office in this building for many years. In addition, the building housed a dining room during World War II. It was recently torn down.

27. BOWEN RESIDENCE

Burnice P. Bowen ran fishing parties, rented motorboats, and guided duck hunting parties on the Patuxent River and Chesapeake Bay in season. In the early 1900s, Mr. Bowen worked as an officer on the steamboat *Westmoreland*, and was also captain of a Maryland oyster police boat. It is still in use as a private residence.

28. REKAR'S HOTEL (SITE)

This 42-room hotel and restaurant was started in 1922 by William and Mary Rekar and lasted until 1961 when it was torn down. It is said to have had the first rooms on the island with running water. It was leased by the U.S. Navy during World War II to accommodate civilian and military personnel stationed at the Amphibious Training Base (see #79) and the Naval Mine Warfare Test Station (see #73). The navy added the large dormers and the exterior fire escapes on the third floor when that floor housed naval personnel working in the building. A restaurant and motel occupy the site today.

Rekar's Hotel, shortly after World War II, with the J.C. Webster & Co. store on the left.

29. Webster Store (site)

The first store on this site was owned by James F. Lusby. It was then rented by John Fletcher Webster from Deal's Island around 1886. In 1889, John's brother, J. Cook, joined him and the store became J. F. Webster and Bro. J. C. Webster later bought his brother out. In 1924 it became J. C. Webster & Co., owned by J. Cook Webster and his nephews Ormsby P. Webster and Thomas V. Thomas. J. C. Webster died in 1938 having sold his interest to the other two partners.

The business was a combination dry goods, grocery store, and marine supplier, on two floors. The store provisioned boats of all sizes, from bugeyes to naval vessels, and had its own wharf. A big potbellied stove with benches around it was the center of attraction for most of the watermen in the harbor on any given day. Solomons native Charles Elliott recalled in 1995 that he worked in the store in his youth and was

Webster's Store around 1905. Just visible in the background is the small bridge across the tidal inlet, since filled in.

paid one dollar for a seventeen hour day. Among his duties were cleaning up the peanut shells from the floor in the morning following a visit by oyster dredge boat crews the night before. He also picked up supplies from the steamboat wharf with a horse and wagon.

Occupying low ground, the store flooded frequently, a situation aggravated by a nearby tidal pond which flooded its banks in severe nor'easters. During the hurricane of August 1933, water reached within two feet of the counter tops and a rowboat was used inside the store to move goods to higher shelves. Canned foods with labels washed off were sold at special discount prices — potential buyers shaking cans to guess the contents. The store was demolished in 1967 to make room for a motel and bar. However, the handsome Webster family home, built in 1905, still looks out over the river from its site on Patuxent Avenue.

30. EASTERN SHORE TRUST COMPANY (SITE)

The first bank was established on Solomons Island in 1905 in temporary quarters in a former barber shop occupied by the late Benjamin J. Warren; a branch of the Eastern Shore Trust Company of Maryland. The following year, a new small wooden bank building was completed on William Street, next door to the Methodist parsonage. William H. Hellen was the first president

Eastern Shore Trust Company Bank, built in 1925, with, beyond, the "cottage" built for Clarence E. Davis in 1906.

and Halvor H. Hellen, his son, was the first assistant cashier. In later years, Halvor Hellen's son recalled how his father rowed to work from the family home on Hellen's Neck with a horse in tow. Once on the other side he saddled the horse and was on his way.

The bank moved in 1925 to this site on a bluff between the Davis home and Webster's Store. In 1933, following reorganization, it became the County Trust Company. In 1961 it changed to Maryland National Bank, which then moved to Lusby in 1977. Today this structure serves as a gift shop for a nearby marina.

31. MOLS LEG ISLAND

This man–made island was built in 1972 to hold the spoils from a shoal which was all that remained of the original natural island. The island was used by the Hellen family for grazing horses and once featured two small hills and several trees. It also served as a convenient place to dry fishing nets, and sometimes as a "potter's field" for deceased sailors from the United States Public Health Service relief station or "marine hospital" who had no known kin. Asa Ketcham and Philip T. Vail built huge wooden reels to roll their nets on for drying, mending, and tarring. The origin of the name is obscure, although one tradition holds that Mols Leg is a corruption of a Scandinavian phrase meaning "sea bum resting place."

32. DAVIS HOUSE

This was the residence of Clarence E. Davis, son of Marcellus M. Davis, and dates from 1906 when it was built by Messrs. Spicknall and Wells. Davis was owner of the M.M. Davis & Son Shipyard from 1924 until his death in 1936. It is now a bed-and-breakfast inn.

33. CAREY OYSTER SHED (SITE)

Merrill Carey shucked oysters and ran a crab shedding business in a small shed on this site. He sold oysters from his leased beds to local residents and businesses. Customers, however, had to pick up their purchases. He often shucked and donated oysters to local churches for their oyster suppers. One side of the building was used by Dr. Reginald V. Truitt of the Chesapeake Biological Laboratory to carry out oyster and plankton experiments

Carey Oyster Shed with Mols Leg Island in the distance. Note the trees on the island, prior to the 1933 storm.

between 1922 and 1925, until larger facilities were obtained for the laboratory.

34. CALVERT ICE COMPANY (SITE)

The Calvert Ice Company was incorporated in 1897 and in the same year an ice house was built by James T. and Charles L. Marsh on land leased from the estate of English, Maltby, and Farren. The lot was described as starting "fifteen feet from the northwest corner of the slaughter house." A slaughterhouse is marked on the 1893 plat of Solomons Island (not to be confused with the one in Avondale, see #49).

The ice house was a welcome addition. Blocks of ice were shipped in from Havre de Grace, Crisfield, and New England, and stored on the site until needed. Ice was a necessity for local seafood packers. It was also cut and distributed by wagon for storage in people's wooden iceboxes. Elliot Dixon, who delivered much of the ice, was well known to everyone in the community. He also hired himself out for plowing, and stabled the horses of visiting "drummers," or traveling salesmen. One of his other jobs was repairing the oyster shell roads on the island. A specially designed wagon with movable slats in the bottom allowed oyster shells to fall through into the hole to be filled.

The company did not prosper however, and the building was sold at auction in 1902 for $245. On a 1913 road plat the site is labeled as the "old ice plant." In 1922 new articles of incorporation were taken out and a new plant built on lots 104 and 105, the same as the original site. This plant was engaged in the manufacture of ice in 100–pound blocks using a compressor run by a one–cylinder diesel engine.

The Calvert Ice Company continued manufacturing into the 1950s when refrigerated trucks and home refrigerators caused its closure. It was sold to G. I. Rupert Lore in 1955 and burned in an electrical fire in December 1958. It is on the present site of Harbor Island Marina.

35. Swift's Ferry Terminal (site)

Capt. Ed Swift came to Solomons from Virginia in 1915 to fish pound nets. When the fishing declined in the late teens, he established a ferry service between Solomons and Millstone Landing on the St. Mary's side of the Patuxent River. It operated from 1920 to 1933. Using his sharp–ended fishing boat, he towed a small scow on which he could load one automobile. Around 1925, he had a larger boat built at the M. M. Davis Shipyard along the lines of an open launch. Named for his son, Otho, it carried passengers under a canopy–type cover and towed a larger scow on which several automobiles could be loaded. The new boat cost $1,106.16 to build. With skilled maneuvering of the *Otho*, Swift could swing the scow around and

Swift's Ferry "Otho," built around 1925. Passengers rode under the canopy while the scow on left was towed behind with automobiles.

back it into the shore where a ramp was lowered for unloading the cars. There was no schedule; service was provided on demand. During the hurricane of August 1933, the ferry was driven up the Narrows and service was discontinued shortly thereafter. A new service was established in 1934 by John Quincy Adams of Virginia out of Capt. Joseph Rodie Langley's dock (see #6).

36. Isaac Solomon Oyster Canning Company (site)

Established in 1867, this was the first canning operation on the island. The exact location is lost in time although it did have a large single-story building about four hundred feet long with a "T" extending out over the water. The center section was two stories, contained an office, and was topped by a cupola and flag staff. Here the Patuxent Lodge of the Knights of Pythias met after the company closed. Solomon's business also included housing for workers and lime kilns for turning shells into fertilizer.

The earliest record of Isaac Solomon's enterprise is found in the *St. Mary's Beacon* of April 9, 1868. In a glowing report, the newspaper states that 1400 bushels of oysters per day were steamed, opened, canned, and prepared for market. Oysters were being shipped as far away as California and Australia. The report went on to say that the waters around Solomons Island contained "an almost inexhaustible supply of oysters of superior quality." The factory and the island were bought by Farren and Moore in 1879; the factory was operated under the name J. S. Farren & Company (Farren holding two-thirds interest) for only a few years before it closed down. Most of the canning company's buildings had disappeared by 1890 through a combination of neglect and storm damage.

37. Town Hall/Machine Shop/Shirt Factory (site)

In 1893 a storehouse was built on this site for owner B. H. Farren to take the place of an old one nearer the steamboat wharf. The first town hall was located on the second floor where it was used for meetings and entertainment. The storeroom was on the first floor. The town hall was later moved to the Parish Hall (see #40). A machine shop replaced the storeroom on the first floor and a Mr. Bacon established a shirt factory on the second floor. By the 1920s large piles of oyster shells could be found nearby which caused this part of the island to be known as "Shell Pile." Oyster shells were brought by truck from the J. C. Lore and Sons Oyster House (see #2). In the spring shells were loaded onto boats and spread on state-owned oyster bars.

38. Steamboat Wharf (site)

Here the steamboats landed to discharge and receive passengers and freight. The first steamer landed here in 1866; the first wharf was built in 1890. Prior to this date steamboats merely came alongside the point, with its deep water, and used a gangplank to get freight and passengers on and off. In 1906 the steamboat wharf was enlarged and repaired "which is necessary to hold such enormous crowds as flock to meet the nightly steamer" (*Calvert Journal*, Aug. 11, 1906).

A 1913 road plat shows this wharf as being used by the Maryland, Delaware and Virginia Railway Company. Another wharf, just up the harbor, serviced the Maryland Steamboat Company, but it was often used to ship bushel baskets of tomatoes to market, giving it the name "tomato wharf." Regularly scheduled steamboating ended in 1935, although occasional excursion steamers made port up until the 1950s.

Waiting for the steamboat in the early 1920s. In the background, left of center, is the Calvert Ice Company plant (courtesy, The Mariners' Museum, Newport News, VA).

The site of the steamboat wharf is currently used by boats of the Chesapeake Biological Laboratory's fleet (see #45).

39. THE OLD SOLOMONS HOUSE

Said to date from about 1780, this structure is probably the home shown on an 1814 map drawn by naval hero Commodore Joshua Barney. The large central cross-gable was added to the front roof slope in the early twentieth century. It is the oldest structure in Solomons and is currently part of the Chesapeake Biological Laboratory.

40. The Pump Trees and Parish House/Town Hall (site)

Between these now-massive German lindens, or basswood trees, was the town pump. Under their shade, townsfolk often gathered to escape the summer heat — old men whittled, boys shot marbles, and little girls played with dolls.

The Episcopal parish rectory, a lovely Victorian-era house, once stood here. To its right, looking from Charles Street, stood a two-story Parish House, built in 1906-1907, where community as well as church activities took place. The first public library was located here where for one dollar a year patrons could take out one book a week. Plays were held on the second floor using local talent along with occasional traveling shows. At some point the second floor, complete with stage and dressing rooms, became the town hall. From 1927 to 1939 the Solomons High School graduations were held here. In the early 1930s, Mr. Haney opened Solomons' first movie theater in this "auditorium." High school students walked down the aisles at intermission selling confectionery.

The second floor was made into a complete gym around 1912 by the Reverend Benjamin E. Lovett, Episcopal rector. The first high school classes were held here from 1921-1924. Dr. R. V. Truitt used portions of it for his laboratory when his work outgrew Merrill Carey's shack, and J. C. Webster used portions as a warehouse for his store. The building was demolished around 1955, but some of the lumber was reused in a bungalow in Avondale.

A hot summer's day and some residents are gathered in the shade of the pump trees. To the right is the Episcopal rectory and adjacent parish house.

Across the road from the Parish Hall was a general store and ice cream parlor run by Thomas and Bertie Saunders. Joseph C. Lore Jr. recalled in 1990 that you could get all the ice cream you could eat for a dime. In the 1930s a men's club was located here that was used by crew on the Standard Oil Company fleet (see #93).

41. Store/Can Factory/USMHS Relief Station (site)

Just to the north, on the corner of Charles and William Streets, was a large rectangular building that may have been constructed as the east wing of Isaac Solomon's original cannery (see #36).

It had a variety of uses. By 1893 it served as the home of the third class relief station established by the U.S. Marine Hospital Service to tend to the medical need of crews on vessels in Solomons Harbor. Sometime after 1902, the station moved to a new site (see #44).

The building also served as a tin shop where shipping cans and lard tins were made. In 1906 it was a general store run by Goodman Goldstein (also spelled "Goldstine" at that time), who also had a similar business in Prince Frederick. The building operated as a general store up into the 1920s, and may have been the last part of Isaac Solomon's cannery to survive. Gus and Sam Becker were later proprietors.

The "marine hospital" in 1902, located in what may have originally been part of Isaac Solomon's cannery. The relief station moved in 1903 and the building became a general store.

In the late 1920s the old building was replaced by a smaller two–story one with a double porch which was also used as a general store, with living quarters above and a gas pump outside. It is now a laundromat, with the porches removed and brick and modern siding covering the original clapboard construction.

42. Hotel Northampton/Northam Hotel (site)

The Hotel Northampton was built for William E. and Lorenzo D. Northam and opened for business in 1902. This sixteen-room boarding house, with its distinctive dormers, became the home-away-from-home for business travelers and visiting

Handsome boarding house and residence of the Northam family, built in 1902.

officials. At some point its name was changed to Northam Hotel. By 1907 it was no longer a hotel and had become a private residence in the Northam family until it was sold around 1959. It is the current site of one of the Chesapeake Biological Laboratory buildings on the corner of Charles and William Streets.

43. First Schoolhouse/Knights of Pythias Hall (site)

It is said that the first school building was an old log structure moved by scow from Mill Mount near the head of Mill Creek. A new school was built in 1882 farther north on the island (see #8). In 1889 the Patuxent Lodge of the Knights of Pythias built a 24-foot x 36-foot two-story building on this lot, sometimes known as Castle Hall. Lodge members met on the second floor while the hall below was available for rent. The tall flagstaff atop the building was a well-known mark for local mariners. The lodge, organized in 1877, previously had its headquarters on the second floor of the old Isaac Solomon Cannery building (see #36). It survived into the 1950s although the building had lain empty many years. In the early years of the twentieth century, the first floor was used as a sail loft by Capt. Olie Olsen (see #60) . In 1899 Charles Anderson used it for the same purpose.

44. "Marine Hospital" (Relief Station)/Solomons Library (site)

The U. S. Marine Hospital Service established a "third class relief station" in Solomons in October 1890 to attend the needs of mariners in the region. Dr. William H. Marsh was appointed acting assistant surgeon in 1890 and held the position until he retired in August of 1930. The marine hospital was moved several times in its early history, but in 1903 settled into this building which was specifically constructed for its use. It stayed here until it closed in 1930. It primarily served the medical needs of crews aboard dredge boats during the oyster season. Dr. Marsh started a library in this building around 1932. It is now a private residence.

45. Chesapeake Biological Laboratory

This is the oldest, permanent, state–supported marine biological laboratory in continuous use on the East Coast. Founded by Dr. Reginald V. Truitt of the University of Maryland in 1922, the first laboratory was in an oyster shucking shed (see #33). In about 1924 the laboratory moved into the Parish House (see #40). The state of Maryland appropriated money in 1929 for a new building which was dedicated in 1932. Summer classes were offered from 1932 to the early 1940s in

Chesapeake Biological Laboratory in the early 1930s.

conjunction with the Johns Hopkins University, Goucher College, Western Maryland College, St. John's College, and Washington College. The laboratory has expanded today into a number of buildings and also operates several research vessels.

Extending along Farren Avenue where the current CBL facilities are located were a series of two–story duplex dwellings. Believed to be housing built by Isaac Solomon for packing house workers, these buildings survived into the first decade of the twentieth century and were known locally as the "company houses."

46. Marsh House/"The Maples"

Dr. William Henry Marsh, who was acting assistant surgeon for the Marine Hospital Service (see #41, #44), lived here. The first weather station was established on the island in 1892 by Dr. Marsh for the U.S. Weather Bureau. His wife, Mary E., whom everybody called "Miss Mollie," frequently took in boarders at "The Maples." In 1898, weekly rates were $5 and the boarding house advertised large airy rooms with no mosquitoes. One notable boarder was Hulbert Footner, who married Marsh's daughter Gladys. He later lived at the historic house he named "Charles Gift," and became a well-known Maryland writer. Marsh's other daughter, Edna, married Clarence E. Davis, who owned M. M. Davis Shipyard. Dr. Marsh had an office in the rear of his residence where he saw patients.

47. Sunset View or Elliott's Inn (site)

This boarding house and restaurant was established in 1915 by Mr. John Elliott, a ship carpenter. At that time there were no buildings between it and the Patuxent River to block the beautiful view, particularly at sunset. This thirty-room house provided room and board to shipyard workers, sports fishermen, and vacationers until World War II. During the war it housed naval personnel until the barracks at the Amphibious Training Base (see #79) were completed. Thereafter it accommodated wives of servicemen stationed in the area. It remained in the family as a boarding house until the 1960s and as a residence until 1991, when it was sold and torn down.

Avondale (Johnstown) in the early 1900s. Prominent in the center is the "Bridge House," and to its right the old bridge to Solomons Island.

AVONDALE/JOHNSTOWN

Until the early 1890s, the residents of Solomons lived almost entirely on the island, with a few families on the adjacent Dowell peninsula and on farms north of the island. Most of the farmland immediately north of the island was owned by the Somervell family, but during the 1870s its status was unclear pending the outcome of a court case to determine the disposition of property to the heirs of Alexander Somervell who died in 1865. Land from the east of the public road to Back Creek eventually went to daughter Emma Sedwick who named her 250-acre holdings as Clair's Point farm. Emma Sedwick died in 1884 leaving four young children, and it was soon necessary to arrange the sale of the farm. Although the lawyer appointed as trustee could not sell the entire farm, he did realize that there would be a market for building lots immediately north of the island. Accordingly, he had forty-two acres laid out into eighty-seven lots as a development to which he gave the name "Avondale." By 1901 he had sold thirty-nine lots, then "selling" the remaining land back to the heirs who were then of age.

The Avondale area soon became better known locally as "Johnstown," named for one of its more colorful residents, John Olsen, who reputedly built the first house. (The name "Johnstown" still appears on modern navigational charts, but it is "Avondale" on official tax records.) Many houses from the 1890s and early twentieth century remain in Avondale, but many are modified. Additional houses were built in the 1930s as vacation rentals; other houses have been built in recent years.

North of the original Avondale area — which ended at the present-day Langley Lane — a large farm of one hundred acres was sold in 1903. By 1919 it was resold and then divided into building lots, several of which were sold to the county in 1924 for the Solomons School — now the site of the Calvert Marine Museum. Prior to World War II, much of the area north of the school was fields for such crops as tomatoes. A cannery was also located in this area on the edge of Back Creek. Following World War II, a small shopping center was built, followed in subsequent years by another shopping center, marinas, restaurants, and motels. Little of the original farmland is discernible today.

The area to the west of Solomons Island Road (Route 2), although across from Avondale, was not part of the original subdivision, but it too had been owned by the Somervell family in the second half of the nineteenth century. Its subsequent history included farming, a hotel, a planned summer development, and a naval facility in World War II.

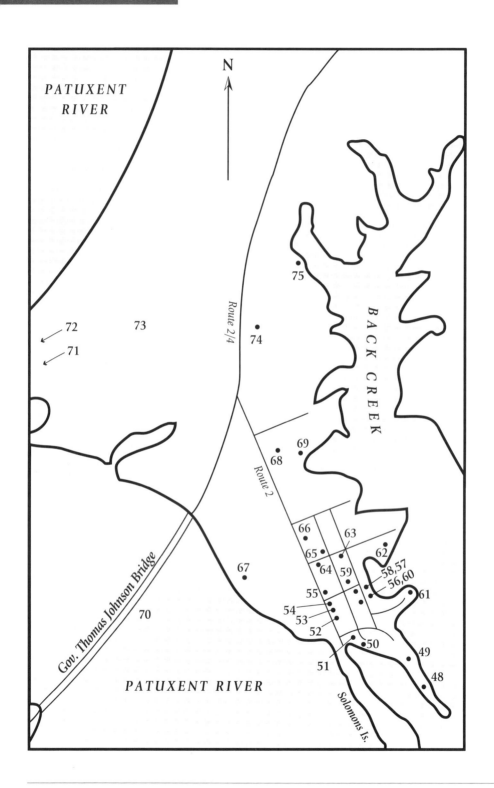

48. LANGLEY MARINA (SITE)/TOWN CENTER MARINA

In 1952 Harry Lee Langley capitalized on the post–World War II boom in recreational boating by building a marine railway and marina on a seven acre site at the end of Clair's Point, with slips for 75 boats. It is the current site of Town Center Marina. Prior to this date he operated a marina at Langley Point, at the end of Lore Street (now Shepherd's Yacht Yard).

H. L. Langley was a dealer for boats made by Owens of Baltimore and later Cruis-Along of Solomons.

49. SLAUGHTERHOUSE (SITE)

A slaughterhouse was located here from 1900 to 1915. Joe Gibson slaughtered one week for J. Cook Webster and then Wilson W. Dowell slaughtered the next. Dowell had his own store on Mill Creek (see #77). In the 1890s, Francis P. Harten had a slaughterhouse and butcher shop that was probably located on the island. For many years meat was delivered by wagon to local residents.

Also located on Clair's Point was a fish house, on the Narrows, and a crab shedding business run by Jack Railey, but little is known about these activities.

50. FLOUR MILL/ICE HOUSE (SITE)

In 1904 the Calvert Milling and Manufacturing Company of New Jersey leased land on this site, known as the "Factory Lot," from John F. and Thomas B. Webster for the purposes of building a grist mill.

By April 1906 construction had started on a three–story wooden structure by Messrs. Spicknall and Wells, who built many homes and businesses in the area at the time. The mill measured thirty–two feet by forty–six feet, and directly in front of it, on the wharf, was the grain elevator with a capacity of 10,000 bushels. Associated with the mill and directly behind it was an ice plant where ice was manufactured using water from an artesian well. It had a daily capacity of five tons, with storage room for one hundred tons of ice.

The steam–powered mill became a landmark in the harbor and its whistle could be heard at regular hours. It was located about where Our Lady Star of the Sea Catholic Church School is now (see #51), and part of it was built out over the waters of the Narrows.

Mr. J. D. Northam was the manager of the ice plant. He occasionally had an open house where visitors could see beautiful red roses and fish frozen into great blocks of ice. Local residents also obtained ice during the winter, using large saws to cut ice from nearby "ice ponds."

Willis E. Overton, originally of Reedville, Virginia, is recorded to have been an owner of the mill and ice plant but details are vague. Overton and his brother had a grocery store in Johnstown in 1887, which was still in business in 1906, but the exact site is unknown. In 1899 they also had a second store near the steamboat wharf.

The mill and ice plant were not long-term economic successes. By the early 1920s the mill had ceased operating and was already becoming dilapidated. It shortly disappeared completely. How long the ice plant was in operation is unknown, but by 1922 the new ice company on the island (see #34) was supplying local needs.

After the closure of the plant, the artesian well was still used on hot summer afternoons for cows from nearby Strathmore Farm to come to refresh themselves.

51. Our Lady Star of the Sea

The parish was established in 1888. The first church was located northeast of here at the cemetery (see #58). It is said the church was started when Jesuits came to Calvert County to preach to the Union forces stationed here during the Civil War. Prior to the erection of the first church, Catholics were served by priests from Benedict, eighteen miles upriver. In 1920 the Church gained its first resident pastor, Father Maurice B. Alexander, and ceased to be a mission of Benedict. It was due to his fundraising efforts that land was

For eight years the old Catholic church (on the right) and the new stood side by side until the former burned in 1936.

acquired on Clair's Point for the site of a new church. He purchased the "Bridge House" on the corner of Avenue A and the state road in 1924. This subsequently became the first rectory. When the present church was dedicated in 1928, its tall steeple gave watermen a new "mark" to use for location of "rocks" (oyster bars) on the Patuxent River. The church school was started in 1933.

52. AUNT MAME'S ROOMS (SITE)

Run by Mary M. Woodburn, wife of Harry M. Woodburn — and known to everyone as Aunt Mame — this establishment operated by word-of-mouth from the 1930s until 1959. She frequently took the overflow when nearby boarding houses were full. Guests included numerous fishing parties and actors from the Floating Theatre when in town. A regular visitor was a young radio announcer named Arthur Godfrey.

53. "AVONDALE"/MILLINERY/SOMERVELL STORE (SITE)

Willis E. Overton and his wife Samantha purchased this lot circa 1892 from the Sedwick estate and built an imposing home; James T. Marsh cut and sawed the lumber for the building.

A few years later, the Overtons opened a grocery and general merchandise store on the property. In 1909 Mrs. William Somervell and family moved into the house and kept the store. Her daughter, Marie Somervell Condiff, also had a millinery shop here.

While still owned by the Overtons, the house was run by John W. and Bessie Marsh as a summer boarding house named "Avondale." By 1906 Marie and William H. Condiff were operating it as a boarding house. Room and board was available during the 1930s for about $10 a week. The Condiffs moved the store to the back of the lot where it is still in use as a garage and storeroom. The house is now a private residence.

"Avondale" boarding house, from a postcard.

54. Joseph Cobb Lore House

Joseph C. Lore Sr. came to Solomons from New Jersey in 1888 and founded the J. C. Lore Company (see #2). In 1890 he married Sarah Jane Tucker, daughter of prosperous waterman Lemuel J. Tucker, and from this union seven sons and two daughters were born. J. C. Lore bought the property for $150 in 1896 and built the present house on the site the same year. Behind the main house is a small building that was Kenneth ("Gus") Lore's first store where he sold confectionery and ice cream. Gus Lore moved his business to the property just south of the J. C. Lore Oyster House where he also had a sandwich shop until the late 1930s. A two-story store was later built on the site which became the location of the post office in 1958 (see #24).

55. Solomons Variety Store/Woodburn's Food Market (site)

This was the site of the well-known Woodburn's Food Market, operated by Benjamin "Dick" Woodburn and later his son, Edgar, until it was torn down in 1989. From about 1936 it was known as Solomons Variety Store, run by Ben Shockett and later Sylvan Rubin. Owners before Shockett included Norval Dixon and Elliott Dixon, who operated it as a general store. Norval Dixon's father built the store and Norval himself was born here in 1916. A retail complex called the Avondale Center is located there today.

56. Elliot Store/Saghy Shoe Repair (site)

James Edward ("Jim Ed") Elliott operated a single-story general store here from before World War I. Part of it was later used as a shoe repair shop by Louis Saghy who was in business from around 1930 until 1942. Mr. Saghy also custom-made shoes for people who needed corrective or special shoes. Born in Austria-Hungary, Saghy emigrated to the U.S. in 1904 on the German liner *Kronprinzessen Cecilie*. On a return voyage to get his wife he came back on the *Kaiser Wilhelm II*. Both of these ships ended up in the "Ghost Fleet" mothballed in the Patuxent River (see #72). Saghy's first daughter Mary was born on the *Kaiser Wilhelm II*. Mrs. Saghy was well known for her dill which she grew in the yard. The Saghys came to Solomons from Baltimore and returned there in 1940. The old Elliott store on Calvert Street has been torn down.

57. Lusby Inn (site)

During the 1920s this house was operated as a boarding house by Everett Lusby. Chartered fishing parties were also available, run by his son Guy. It has since been torn down.

58. OUR LADY STAR OF THE SEA (SITE) AND CEMETERY

This cemetery marks the original site of St. Mary's Star of the Sea Catholic Church (later Our Lady Star of the Sea), built in 1895. In the 1920s this church building was moved to the present site of the parochial school of Our Lady Star of the Sea (see #51).

The first Catholic church, on its original site, around 1910.

Moving the church was a community effort that cut across religious lines. Under the direction of Capt. Joseph Rodie Langley, the building was jacked up and a wooden sled built underneath that rested on heavily-greased 12 by 12 inch oak timbers laid in the direction of movement. A stump puller or windlass was set ahead of the church, connected by strong cables. Two heavy draft horses turned the windlass and the building slid slowly forward. It was a laborious job as the timbers and windlass had to be moved repeatedly to keep ahead.

Tragically, after all the effort, the building burned in 1936, destroying many of the older church records.

59. BARBER SHOP (SITE)

Alex Railey operated a barber shop on this site from about 1924 until the late 1930s. Barbering was done in the evenings and weekends as Railey worked at the M. M. Davis Shipyard during the day. When he stopped barbering he tore the shop down and built small skiffs as a sideline.

60. Olsen Sail Maker Shop (site)

On this site Olaf Olsen owned a small building, up the hill from his dock, where he repaired sails and made rigging. In the 1920s and 1930s, he and his wife Cora ran a boarding house, built in 1906, and organized charter fishing parties. Olsen's father was John Olsen, Johnstown's first resident (see #61).

61. John Olsen House

Capt. John M. Olsen of Norway came to America by sailing ship in 1885. He became a successful waterman and built a house, the first on the mainland north of Solomons, about 1890. Consequently, the area became known locally as "John's town" (Johnstown was originally named Avondale).

Olsen maintained the navigation beacons at Point Patience and Sandy Point. With his flat-bottomed skiff, he rowed out to each beacon and filled the kerosene lanterns every other day. For some unknown reason, he always rowed his 16-foot skiff facing forward.

John Olsen became a well-known fixture of the Solomons waterfront and

John Olsen with striped bass.

according to some accounts, established a name for decorative marine carvings. Today, the Calvert Marine Museum is home to a local chapter of the American Shipcarver's Guild.

In 1904 Olsen tore down his original residence and built a new, three-story house on the site. His former home is still a private residence.

62. HASKELL CRAB HOUSE (SITE)/LORE'S RAILWAY (SITE)/ ZAHNISER'S SAILING CENTER

Most of this property was originally owned by Lemuel J. Tucker, whose daughter, Sarah Jane Tucker, married Joseph C. Lore Sr. in 1890. L. J. Tucker acquired the property in 1900 and sold it to his daughter in 1917. In this manner it passed into the Lore family.

Capt. Russell D. Haskell, a retired ship's master, opened a crab house on this site around 1931. Crab meat was shipped to market by truck, after being steamed and picked. When James Osborn Lore took over the property in 1936, he tore down the crab house and operated a general repair yard with two marine railways and machine shop, which lasted until about 1944. During the Second World War, the U.S. Navy leased the yard for maintenance and repair of landing craft used at the Naval Amphibious Training Base. In 1960 the property became A. W. Zahniser & Son Marina and Boatyard and, in 1970, Zahniser's Sailing Center. Since it began, the company has conducted general repair work as well as building boats. The barn-type structure at the head of the marine railway was J. O. Lore's boatbuilding shed.

Two lots over from the Haskell crab house, John Glover built rowing skiffs and sold them for one dollar per foot in the years before World War II.

63. SHIRT FACTORY (SITE)

Walter Lusby managed a shirt factory on this site between 1922 and 1924 for Mr. Keating, a Singer Sewing Machine salesman. Keating started his business (the Olivet Manufacturing Co.) at Olivet in the old church hall but moved to Solomons and built a larger building. He operated a bus service between Olivet and Solomons for benefit of his workers.

Approximately thirty women were employed at the Avondale Manufacturing Company. Skipper Dixon ran the gas engine that worked the belt-driven sewing machines. An earlier factory was located in the old town hall near the steamboat wharf (see #37). The building in Avondale burned Christmas morning 1925. Two bungalows presently on the site were reportedly built from materials salvaged from the factory.

64. CHESAPEAKE AND POTOMAC TELEPHONE COMPANY BUILDINGS/ TONGUE HOUSE

The Chesapeake and Potomac Telephone Company installed community dial equipment on this site on August 13, 1935, the first dial system in Calvert County. These two buildings were built by Frank Tongue and leased to C & P for twenty-five years. The first telephone was installed by the Baltimore, Chesapeake and Annapolis Telephone Company in 1899, and by 1906 a number of local businesses and prominent citizens were connected to the outside world by this new marvel of the age.

The C & P buildings at the rear of the Tongue house in 1995.

The Tongue family house was built by Capt. James O. Tongue in 1905 with lumber he brought by schooner from Salisbury, on the Eastern Shore. As a gift, the lumber merchant gave Captain Tongue a fireplace mantel and an etched glass door panel, which can be seen in the house today. It is still owned by the Tongue family.

65. POLLING HOUSE (SITE)

The Solomons Polling House was located on Sedwick Avenue on the northeast corner of this property. This polling house was in place by 1906 and was moved from its original site on William H. Hellen's property on the Dowell peninsula according to the *Calvert Gazette* of September 16, 1905. For the November 1905 elections a temporary polling house was set up in a house adjoining G. Goldstein's store (see #41). This proved to be a mixed blessing, as the Solomons correspondent for the *Calvert Journal* of November 11, 1905, recorded:

> While it may be progressive, and convenient for our residents, there are undesirable features about it, as it draws crowds on our quiet streets of different elements.

By 1906 citizens from Olivet, Mill Creek (Dowell), and Rousby Hall voted here because it was more convenient for them to come by boat than to walk or ride a carriage to the town of Frazier (now Appeal).

The small rectangular building with two doors and two windows has since been torn down.

66. VAIL HOUSE

This Queen Anne–style house was built in 1906 by Charles Spicknall of Lower Marlboro for Capt. Philip T. Vail who came to Solomons from Oyster Bay, Long Island, New York. The lumber was brought across the Bay from Salisbury in the log canoe *Amelia*. It was one of the first houses in the area to have central heating. The bowed windows, expensive even today, were broken during mine and torpedo testing on the Patuxent during World War II. All the molding used inside is of American holly. Captain Vail was a successful pound net fisherman setting ten to twelve nets from Cove Point to below Cedar Point. Numerous men were employed in cutting net stakes, skinning off bark, driving poles, hanging nets, and hauling

Vail House under construction in 1906.

fish. A major pound net repair and tarring facility was operated by Vail just north of Drum Point Pond (see #91). Captain Vail's twelve-year-old son Kenneth was killed in 1904 on the steamboat wharf at Solomons when a hawser thrown from the steamer *St. Mary's* caused a derrick on the wharf to fall on young Vail. Preston Woodburn (see #4) and his family lived here after the Vails moved out. It is presently known as Holiday Manor, a private residence.

67. STRATHMORE FARM

Originally owned by the Somervell family and later by Daniel Overton and J. C. Webster (1901), this farm supplied milk, meat, and vegetables for the Webster store (see #29) as well as growing wheat and corn. Wilbur T. Grover was the long-time farm manager. The dairy, which operated from 1938 to 1942, had its own milk

James L. "Pepper" Langley poses around 1934 with the Strathmore Dairy delivery van, which he had recently lettered.

bottles stamped "Strathmore Dairy, Solomons, Md." A large Victorian farmhouse, built in the 1880s by Louisa Somervell Solomon (Charles S. Solomon's wife) was torn down in 1957. The property is now owned by grandchildren of Mr. Webster.

On the riverbank of Strathmore Farm, just to the west of the tidebox (see #1), was a point of land that was known as Smallpox Point. According to older residents, it was here that victims of this dreaded disease were buried.

68. CALVERT MARINE MUSEUM

This building was first the Solomons Elementary and High School, and now continues its educational purpose as part of the Calvert Marine Museum. Built in 1925, the structure served as the first lower Calvert County consolidated elementary school from 1925 until 1972, and as the high school from 1925 until 1939. Local citizens raised the money to purchase the four acre plot — the building itself cost $21,500. Leaving behind their one-room schools, wooden outhouses marked "Girls" or "Boys," water buckets with dipper, and the one teacher, students from Dowell, Olivet, and Rousby boarded the schoolboat *James Aubrey* for the trip to their new school. Here were central heating, water fountains, indoor lavatories, and a teacher in each classroom (electricity was installed later). Part of the basement was later converted into a cafeteria.

The schoolboat operated from 1925 until 1935 under the command of Capt. Isaac "Ike" H. Hill, with his son Wilson as engineer. *James Aubrey* was one of the few schoolboats in operation east of the Mississippi in the early twentieth century. It was originally built as a sailing brogan (two–masted, partially decked–over canoe) for fishing and oystering, then converted to a gas–screw passenger vessel by the M. M. Davis shipyard of Solomons in 1925. The flagpole in front of the museum is said to be the mast taken from the *James Aubrey* during this conversion. Captain Hill obtained a contract with the school board for $1,750 to carry the children of Olivet, Dowell, and Rousby Hall to and from school. The first pick–up was around 7:30 a.m. and the one-way trip, crisscrossing St. John's and Mill Creeks, took about forty-five minutes. The 42–foot schoolboat had a cabin built over its entire length and was divided into three compartments: a pilot house, a passenger section with benches along each side and down the middle, and an engine room. A small wood-burning stove was set up just aft of the pilot house for heat when needed. When the ice was too thick on the creeks, the children walked to school. The water community students identified themselves as "up–creekers" and the non–water community children as "up–roaders." Competition in school games was often between these two groups. All that remains of this interesting era, other than the *James Aubrey* mast, is some rotted pilings from the old school pier, still visible next to the seawall near the Drum Point Lighthouse at Calvert Marine Museum.

Archie Woodburn driving the West Shore Transit Company bus in front of the Solomons Elementary and High School, sometime after 1925.

The old schoolhouse was declared surplus property in 1972 after serving as the Solomons School for forty–seven years. The property was leased to the Calvert County Historical Society in 1973, and was opened to the public on June 29, 1975, as the Calvert Marine Museum, which had been in a temporary building on the island (see #3). After the museum's Exhibition Building was opened in 1989, the old schoolhouse was again closed. It reopened in 1993 as the museum's Administration Building.

69. DRUM POINT LIGHTHOUSE

Built in 1883 at Drum Point, the confluence of the Patuxent River with the Chesapeake Bay, the light was decommissioned by the U.S. Coast Guard in 1963. The prefabricated structure took thirty–three days to build at a cost of $25,000. The light was a fixed red beacon; the fog bell was rung in bad weather by a six–hundred–pound weight–driven, mechanical bell striker which struck a double blow every

Drum Point Lighthouse in 1961, two years before it was decommissioned (courtesy, United States Coast Guard).

fifteen seconds. Referred to as a cottage–style, screwpile light, it was one of forty–two screwpile lighthouses built on the Chesapeake Bay. Of these, only four survive today. The lighthouse was moved to the museum in 1975, restored to its early twentieth century appearance, and opened to the public on June 24, 1978.

70. GOV. THOMAS JOHNSON BRIDGE

This bridge was named for the first governor of the state of Maryland, leader of the American Revolution in Maryland, and friend of George Washington. He was born a few miles north of here on the shores of St. Leonard Creek. The bridge connects Calvert and St. Mary's Counties, has a height of 140 feet, and spans water depths up to 123 feet. The bridge was dedicated and opened to the public in December 1977 making the ferry operation (see #6) obsolete.

71. POINT PATIENCE

In 1661, the 360-acre patent known as Point Patience was acquired by John Ashcomb. The original Ashcomb house, then owned by John Parran, was burned by the British in 1780. It was rebuilt and burned again by the British in 1814, at which time it was owned by a Dr. William D. Somervell. Point Patience is a long sandy neck projecting into the Patuxent River. During the era of sail, vessels had a difficult time navigating around this obstacle and usually waited for favorable tide and wind — hence the name. In 1678 the Provincial Council of the colony decreed that a ferry should be established at Ashcomb's Plantation. Since Town Point is directly across the river from Point Patience, the assumption is that the ferry linked these two points. The ferry existed from 1678 until 1694 when it fell into disuse after the capital of the colony was moved from St. Mary's City to Annapolis.

Point Patience was bought by the Marburger family in 1893. John H. Marburger opened a store near the main house in 1898. In a freak accident, the store was destroyed by a "cyclone" in 1899 and Marburger was killed. Mrs. Fannie Marburger operated the home as a summer boarding house by 1898, when rates were one dollar per day or five dollars per week. Billed as "one of the garden spots of Maryland," the resort offered many amenities including dances every night. On August 14, 1909, the local newspaper reported twenty-three boarders staying at the time. Point Patience was sold in 1916 to Thomas Parran, but the home continued to be run as a guest house owned by the Point Patience Hotel and Development Corp. It was known as the Point Patience Hotel in the 1930s.

The appearance of the old house was radically altered when remodeled by Frank and Beulah Tomlinson in 1942, and again in 1943 by the U.S. Navy for the residence of the Commanding Officer of the Naval Mine Warfare Test Station (see #73). The current building sits on the old foundation and includes portions dating back to the 1820s.

72. GHOST FLEET

The deep waters of the protected Patuxent River offered excellent anchorage for mothballed ships. Here, up to six U.S. Shipping Board surplus ships, known as the Ghost Fleet, were moored from 1927–1940. *Kronprinzessen Cecilie* (renamed *Mount Vernon*), *George Washington*, *Kaiser Wilhelm II* (renamed *Monticello*), and *Amerika* (renamed *America*) were former German liners interned during World War I. *American Legion* and *Southern Cross* were built for the U.S. Shipping Board in the 1920s, and laid-up here in 1939. The *George Washington* was refitted and carried President Woodrow Wilson to the peace signing at Versailles, France, in 1918–1919.

The "Ghost Fleet" moored in the Patuxent River, south of Point Patience.

73. SOLOMONS NAVAL MINE WARFARE TEST STATION/RECREATION CENTER

This facility was established in 1942 for testing mines and torpedoes. A hard-hat diving school was also established here to aid in the recovery of ordnance and to take advantage of the 130-feet deep, black waters found at Point Patience for training. An American submarine (S-49) used in ordnance testing still lies in these waters. Over the years two watermen lost their boats as a result of torpedo tests. Controversy between the navy and watermen over fish kills from explosives continued up until the 1960s. For a number of years, starting in 1972, the Empress Radiation Environment Simulator for warship vulnerability to nuclear attacks was located here. The navy now operates the area as a military recreation center.

74. D & L Shopping Center

Built in 1947, this was the first shopping center built in the lower peninsula of Calvert County. Named D & L after Benny Dowell and Jack Laningham, this center once had a bowling alley, movie theater, snack bar, People's Food Store, and the Dowell and Laningham Packard and Studebaker showroom. Other Dowell family members involved in the business included Fulton, Lee, and Charles Dowell.

75. Calvert Packing Company (site)

From about 1925 until 1934 local tomatoes were processed and shipped by boat from here to market under the Leonard Calvert brand. Partners were W. W. Dowell, H. H. Hellen, and H. B. Trueman. Tomatoes were brought to the plant by farm wagon and truck. Local farmer Claude Turner of Lusby shipped his tomatoes by boat from the Spout Farm wharf on St. Leonard Creek to Solomons to be canned at the plant. On one occasion, in protest over the buying price, Mr. Turner dumped all his tomatoes in St. Leonard Creek where the water was red for days around the wharf.

Before the factory was built, tomatoes were taken directly by wagon to the steamboat wharf for shipment to Baltimore. Young boys delighted in jumping on the wagons as they made their way to the wharf and eating as many tomatoes as they could.

Charles L. Marsh and his son, Joseph, with the first oyster tongs patented by Marsh in 1887.

THE SURROUNDING AREA

Although the town of Solomons grew to be the commercial center of southern Calvert County, with the largest population, its history is intertwined with the surrounding communities of Dowell, Olivet, Rousby Hall, and Drum Point. Bordering on Back Creek, Mill Creek, St. John Creek, and the Patuxent River, these areas were inhabited by "up–creekers," as Solomons Island residents often called their neighbors to the north. The land was made up mainly of scattered farms and watermen's homes with here and there a country store or church. Until well into the twentieth century, water was the primary means of access to the outside world. Here, the family names of Dowell, Joy, Dodson, Lusby, and Thomas predominate.

The community of Dowell received its name from W. W. Dowell who moved into the area in the early years of the twentieth century. It officially became a post office in 1926 when Sadie E. Dowell was appointed the first postmaster. But Dowell had been settled by a number of African American families back in the late nineteenth century.

The Dowell peninsula between Back Creek and Mill Creek was chosen by James T. Marsh, a pioneering shipbuilder in the area, for the site of his new shipyard (1872–1917). Many graceful sailing vessels were launched from there. Most of the land on the peninsula was owned by the prosperous Hellen family, whose family seat looked out over the entrance to Solomons Harbor. The construction of the U.S. Amphibious Training Base in 1942 on this property changed the landscape dramatically. Farms and fields gave way to a vast complex of brick and concrete. But by 1944 the wartime tempo had slowed considerably and the base closed the following year. It is now a privately owned marina, but even to the casual observer the surviving wartime structures are still apparent.

Northeast of the Dowell peninsula is Olivet, a small waterfront community which opened its first post office in 1893, but did not have electricity until 1946. Indoor plumbing at that time was an almost unheard–of luxury. Olivet was an isolated village and for many years mail and supplies were brought by boat from Solomons. Even today, it retains much of its character as a waterfront community and has one of the last operating general stores in the county. A number of Olivet residents were employed at the nearby M. M. Davis Shipyard.

The road to Olivet branches off Rousby Hall Road which takes its name from the seventeenth century estate of the same name owned by John Rousby, and built on the neck of land between Mill Creek and the Patuxent River.

In 1890 the property was the subject of a speculative real estate development when the Patuxent City Land and Improvement Co. of New Jersey purchased approximately 200 acres for $30,000 "for the purpose of building a town." A plat drawn the same year shows a yacht harbor and hotel site with an orderly pattern of streets and lots. Some of the street names, like Trenton Avenue, are a present reminder of this ambitious venture whose failure is linked with the failure of the Baltimore and Drum Point Railroad.

Although the development was never a commercial success, the area became the site of several notable businesses, including the Calvert Brick Co. and the well-known M. M. Davis & Son Shipyard. The latter company moved to this site in 1910 from Solomons Island as it needed more space for its growing boatbuilding and repairing activities. From this location were launched commercial sailing craft, tugs, custom designed yachts, mass-produced recreational craft, and vessels for the U.S. Government. Located on Ship Point, at the northern entrance to Solomons Harbor, were two fish processing companies, active at the turn of the century, and a later oyster shell crushing mill.

To the east of Rousby Hall stands Drum Point, once owned by Calvert County's most exotic resident, Frederick L. Barreda, a Peruvian businessman. He built a large Italianate-style mansion on the property in the 1870s. Drum Point was also the proposed site for the southern terminus of the abortive Baltimore and Drum Point Railroad, which raised so many economic hopes during the railroad building boom following the Civil War.

Drum Point gave its name to the lighthouse that was built just offshore in 1883 to guide mariners into the Patuxent River and the sheltered harbor in the lee of Drum Point. The lighthouse is now at the Calvert Marine Museum (see #69). In recent years, modern housing developments have sprung up at Drum Point, replacing the former landscape of gently rolling fields and woodlands.

Schooner "Matchless" of the U.S. Coast and Geodetic Survey alongside the fish processing plant at Ship Point, 1909.

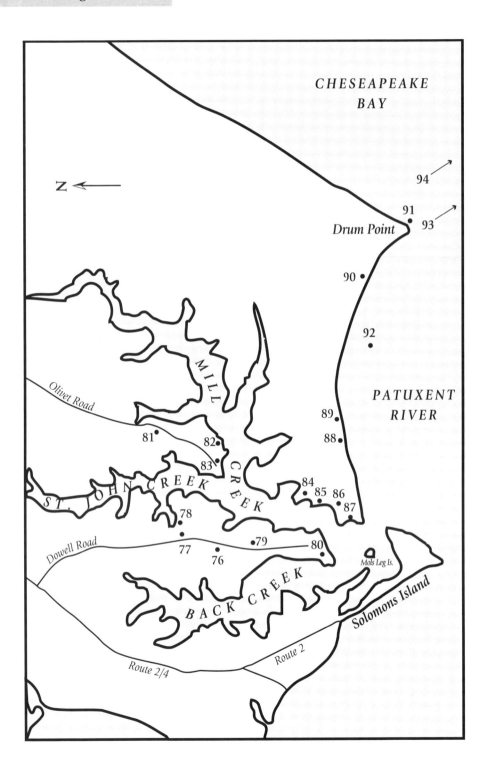

76. DOWELL SCHOOL #12 (SITE)

Located on Dowell Road, the school was built in six weeks in the summer of 1905 for $500. Halvor Hellen was appointed the first teacher on September 19, 1905, and Grace Dorsey in 1906, followed by Lydia Hellen and Ruth Ireland. The school closed in 1925 when all the one–room schools were consolidated at Solomons (see #68).

77. W. W. DOWELL STORE/DOWELL POST OFFICE

The W. W. Dowell Store was started by Wilson W. Dowell who came to this area from Baltimore in the early years of the century. In his youth, he had worked as a waterboy in the construction of the abortive Baltimore and Drum Point Railroad. Wilson W. Dowell was a farmer who also had an interest in vegetable and seafood packing.

Wilson Dowell in front of his general store around 1904.

This building operated as a general store from 1904 to 1983. An early view shows a small 2-1/2 story structure with a shed addition to the right. Over the years it has expanded in several directions but with the living quarters always behind and upstairs in the back.

Dowell officially became a post office in 1926, and it was located in the front, right hand corner of the general store. Today the post office is located in a small building attached to the main store on the left. The latter is now an antique store, still owned by the Dowell family and lovingly preserved with some of the original fixtures still in use.

78. W. W. Dowell Oyster House (site)

Between 1919 and 1937, Wilson W. Dowell had an oyster house where oysters were shucked and then shipped, originally by steamboat from Solomons to Baltimore, but later by truck to Warren Denton Seafood at Broomes Island, where in turn they were taken to Baltimore, also by truck.

The foundations of the oyster house are still visible on the road behind the old W. W. Dowell Store and next to the water.

79. Solomons Naval Amphibious Training Base (site)/Calvert Marina

The U.S. Navy seized 125 acres here in August of 1942 for the nation's first amphibious training base. The nearby Calvert Cliffs and Bay beaches were perfect for mock amphibious assaults. Marines who landed on the beaches of Normandy and the Pacific Solomon Islands were trained here. The U. S. General Services Administration sold the base to the state of Maryland for a marine police headquarters in 1958. It was finally sold and turned into Calvert Marina, now also including condominiums. Thomas W. Moore had a tomato cannery located on the Mill Creek side in 1905–1906 (see #21).

The Amphibious Training Base in 1944. Little of this huge complex now remains (courtesy, U.S. Nat. Archives).

80. James T. Marsh Shipyard/Blacksmith Shop (site)

James T. Marsh came to Solomons from New York after completing an apprenticeship in ship carpentry at the Brooklyn Navy Yard and working in shipyards on Long Island Sound. An unconfirmed story has it that a group of yachtsmen commissioned him to construct a contender for the America's Cup competition. The Chesapeake Bay was an ideal place to secretly design and carry out such an undertaking. Marsh established his shipyard in 1872 across the inner harbor on a peninsula known variously as Hellen's Neck, Mill Creek, or Timber Neck. History does not record the creation of a contending yacht, but Marsh's reputation for building plank–on–frame bugeyes is undisputed. Prior to this innovation (the first recorded

The Marsh shipyard around 1900 with the schooner Martin Sylvester *on the railway for repairs (courtesy, The Mariners' Museum, Newport News, VA).*

frame bugeye was the *Clyde*, built in 1877 by Solomon & Son & Davis at Solomons), bugeyes were built of huge logs, which were then becoming scarce. This, plus Marsh's unfamiliarity with log boat construction, probably contributed to his use of frame construction. The yard had two railways, a steam sawmill, mold loft, and joiner shop as well as a resident sailmaker (Robert Bellows) and rigger. A brother, Charles L. Marsh, inventor of the deep–water patent oyster tongs in 1887, owned a blacksmith shop next door which did all the iron work for the yard. By 1889 business was booming and three skilled workmen were employed at three forges. The Marsh Shipyard was sold at auction in 1917.

Near the yard was a home built in 1809 which was acquired by William H. Hellen in 1845 and lived in continuously by the Hellen family until 1942 when the U.S. Navy bought it for the Solomons Amphibious Training Base. This house was torn down and rebuilt, in modified form, and exists today as the headquarters of the Lord Calvert Yacht Club and Southern Maryland Sailing Association. A curious feature of the house is the large exterior chimney with a window in the middle.

81. Olivet School #10 (site)

The school was opened in 1898 and abandoned in 1925 when the schools all consolidated in Solomons (see #68).

82. Hagelin Store (site)/Dodson's Store

George Hagelin first opened a general store on this site looking out over Mill Creek. By 1918 Joseph E. Joy had acquired the property and built a new store just above the hill behind the old store. The original was kept for a few years until torn down. All merchandise was brought by steamboat to Solomons where it was unloaded and transferred to Olivet by water.

Joseph Joy, who went into politics and was elected to both the Maryland Senate and House of Delegates, ran the store until 1955 when it was leased to James Dodson. Mr. Dodson, who started working at the store in 1937, bought it in 1960 and has run it ever since.

Dodson's Store is a rare survivor of the once common waterfront general store. Little has changed on the inside with the original wood and glass fixtures still in place. Near the stove is a bench that was formerly a pew in the old Olivet Methodist

James Dodson behind the counter of his store in 1995.

Church, which was torn down in 1912 and replaced with the present structure.

83. Lusby Store/Olivet Post Office (site)

William T. Lusby operated a general store at this site from the late 1890s into the 1920s. Mr. Lusby was the postmaster at Olivet until 1922 and used a section of his store for the post office. Olivet was given a post office in 1893, but for many years mail had to be brought to Solomons by boat for onward delivery by steamer. When the building was razed in 1936, the post office was moved into a new building on top of the hill at the road's end. Mr. Lusby's daughter, Sue Dixon, was postmistress from 1922 until 1968. Although now closed, the small building with its porch is a handsome example of a rural waterfront post office.

84. ROUSBY SCHOOL (SITE)

Margaret Condiff was the last teacher at this school. She took the M. M. Davis Shipyard boat from the island to Mill Creek, then walked from the shipyard to the school. After the school consolidation of 1925, this building was relocated to the M. M. Davis Shipyard (see #85) and used as an office. Miss Condiff then became the elementary school principal at the new Solomons School (see #68).

85. DAVIS SHIPYARD AT ROUSBY (SITE)

The M. M. Davis & Son Shipyard (see #13) moved its boatbuilding facilities here in 1910 to accommodate the larger vessels being built at this time. For the new yard, Davis bought at least ten lots from the owners of the Rousby Tract near the Calvert Brick Company operated by Mr. Debelius in the 1900s. Because there were no railroads, all building materials were brought by boat from Baltimore. Later, trucks hauled materials to Solomons where they were transferred to scows and towed to the yard site. A paved road to the yard was not built until 1939. During World War II, expansion to accommodate U.S. Army needs was undertaken, and the company specialized in building 65–foot wooden freight and personnel boats known as T–boats. It subsequently received two Army–Navy "E" awards for outstanding contributions to the war effort.

The Davis yard became most famous for its wooden yacht production during the late 1920s and 1930s, including several well–known racing yachts such as *Seawitch*, *High Tide*, and *Manitou*. After World War II, the yard capitalized on the postwar demand for inexpensive recreational craft by developing the well–known Cruis-Along powerboats, said to be the first assembly–line boats produced for middle-income Americans. The yard closed in 1973 after several changes in ownership. Financial difficulties and competition from fiberglass boats proved insurmountable.

M.M. Davis & Son shipyard about 1930 with a tug and barge under construction.

86. CALVERT BRICK COMPANY (SITE)

The Calvert Brick Company was formed in 1892 on a waterfront site just north of Ship Point after tests made in 1887 reported favorably on the extensive red clay deposits in the area. The following year steam power was installed and bricks were shipped as far away as Florida from the company's wharf on Mill Creek. Closer to home, it supplied the bricks used in building Cedar Point Lighthouse in 1896 and the concrete used in the caisson–style lighthouse at Hooper Island in 1901.

The company changed hands in 1897 and, again, in 1901 when Mr. Debelius, the former superintendent of the company, purchased it and converted it back to making bricks by hand. It stopped operating around 1906 when the red clay deposits became depleted.

87. SHIP POINT

Directly across from the old steamboat wharf site (see #38) lies Ship Point, a part of the original Rousby Hall property. By 1888 a fish processing plant was operating on this site owned by Willis E. Overton and Asa C. Ketcham. In that year the company employed one fish steamer with a crew of sixteen men to deliver the catch. Fourteen thousand fish, called menhaden, were necessary to make one forty–five–gallon barrel of oil. In 1893 Overton patented a fish oil press used by this plant and adopted by other Bay processing plants.

In 1907 J. Cook Webster and William E. Northam built a second fish factory in the same location with Mr. Thomas O. ("Rayne") Tongue as manager. The new enterprise was not entirely welcome in the community, however. The *Calvert Gazette* of June 22, 1907, reported a visit of Benson Bond, county commissioner and the county health officer, to "investigate" the fish factory. "We hope the visit will effect the removal of the obnoxious odor, so annoying to citizens here," commented the Solomons correspondent. In 1911 the business was incorporated as The Patuxent Fish & Oil Company with Asa C. Ketcham, Halvor H. Hellen, and Webster and Northam as directors. Salted herring, herring roe, fertilizer, and fish oil were produced and shipped to Baltimore by steamer. Both factories were operating that year, but in 1927 the Patuxent Fish & Oil Company property was sold for failure to pay taxes. Later, James Osborn Lore erected an oyster shell crushing plant here for the production of lime and chicken feed. Lime was shipped directly to farmers on the Patuxent River using the 52–foot freight boat *Westover*. The plant was destroyed by the August 1933 hurricane.

88. ROUSBY HALL

Rousby Hall takes its name from two brothers, Christopher and John Rousby, who came from England about 1668. Christopher Rousby built "Susquehanna" on the St. Mary's side of the Patuxent River while John called his land "Rousby Hall." John Rousby died in 1685, at the early age of twenty–three, while his brother died the year before in a duel.

The present building dates from around 1818, having been rebuilt on the old foundation after being destroyed by the British during the War of 1812. An earlier building was damaged in 1780 during the Revolutionary War when the owner, Col. William Fitzhugh, denied a British request for provisions.

89. CUSTOMS HOUSE AT ROUSBY HALL

During the eighteenth century this one–story brick structure served as a customs house where ships entering the Patuxent River stopped to pay taxes to the Crown. After falling into ruin, it was recently restored and is now a private residence.

90. BARREDA HOUSE (SITE)

Frederick L. Barreda was the agent in the United States for the Barreda family's Peruvian guano trade. He settled first in Baltimore and became friendly with Richard B. Fitzgerald of Fitzgerald and Booth, and in partnership purchased tracts of land at the mouth of the Patuxent in both Calvert and St. Mary's Counties, including over two thousand acres in the area of Drum Point. At that time, Frederick Barreda lived in New York City and presumably had tenant farmers on the land. He lost most of his fortune in the crash of 1873 and moved with his family to Drum Point where he built a large Italianate–style house, said to be the first house in Calvert County

Barreda House in 1953.

equipped with indoor plumbing. Barreda moved his family to California in the late 1870s, with the large Barreda farm reverting to his brother, Felipe, through default on a mortgage. Although no other Barredas ever lived on Drum Point — all were resident abroad — the property remained in the ownership of the Barreda family until 1942. The house was demolished soon after World War II when the entire Drum Point area began to be developed.

91. DRUM POINT

Forming the north shore of the entrance into the Patuxent River, Drum Point provides a natural lee where sailing vessels frequently waited out bad weather. Drum Point Lighthouse was constructed here in 1883 and relocated to the Calvert Marine Museum in 1975 (see #69).

92. DRUM POINT HARBOR

Drum Point Harbor has been known as an excellent natural harbor since the colonial period. The outer harbor under Drum Point is two miles long and one-and-one-half miles wide with an unobstructed entrance. Water depth is sixty to eighty feet in the middle and shoals gradually to thirty feet within a few hundred yards of shore. Two miles upriver, the Patuxent River turns northward around Solomons Island forming another five miles of anchorage with depths ranging from twenty-six to seventy feet.

As early as 1868 a railroad from Baltimore to Drum Point was contemplated to take advantage of this excellent harbor as a shipping point. By the 1870s, surveying was completed, but not until the 1880s and 1890s was there grading for a portion of the roadbed. Financial difficulties brought a halt to its completion. The dream never died, and between 1911 and 1917 there was a second attempt to complete the Drum Point Railroad. Financial problems and World War I brought it to a final halt.

93. STANDARD OIL COMPANY FLEET

Between 1923 and 1939, three fleets totaling twenty–one Standard Oil tankers were mothballed on the Patuxent off Millstone Landing. The crew from the tanker *Clyde C. Taylor* trained and entered the first American lifeboat team in the International Lifeboat Races. They won the 1933 and 1935 championships and came in second in 1934 and 1936.

Laid-up Standard Oil tankers in the Patuxent River, 1930-1931.

94. PATUXENT RIVER NAVAL AIR STATION

At the outbreak of World War II, the U.S. Navy sought a central location for aviation testing. In 1941 the navy chose 6,400 acres of land at Cedar Point on the southern shore of the Patuxent River as the site for this new facility. The United States Naval Air Station, Patuxent River, Maryland, was commissioned on April 1, 1943. Since then the navy has conducted flight tests to evaluate the flying qualities and performance of military aircraft. In addition, since 1945 pilots have trained at the Naval Air Station's Test Pilots' School. It is currently home of the Naval Air Warfare Center Aircraft Division.

Selected Additional Readings

There are no published histories of Solomons Island and the adjacent area, although there are general histories of Calvert and St. Mary's Counties and events on the Patuxent River. This reading list contains these general histories, as well some other works that have some references to Solomons and those activities — boatbuilding, naval presence, oystering, steamboats, and local scenes — that figured in its 130-year history. A few other works include more history of times pre-dating the beginning of the development of the island following Isaac Solomon's purchase in 1865. Finally, there are a few works of fiction that include the Solomons area as part of their locale. All of these works are available for examination in the Calvert Marine Museum library, and many are also available in the public libraries of Southern Maryland.

General Works

Brooks, Kenneth F. "An Island of the Mind," *Chesapeake Bay Magazine*, September 1974, pp. 9-15, 31. Article about the island in Solomons harbor in the early 1930s.

Cole, Merle T. *Cradle of Invasion: A History of the U. S. Naval Amphibious Training Base, Solomons, Maryland, 1942–45*. Solomons: Calvert Marine Museum, 1984, 37 pp.

————. *The Happy Solution: A Short History of the* Dewey *Floating Dry Dock*. Solomons: Calvert Marine Museum, 1988, 36 pp.

————. *The Patuxent "Ghost Fleet," 1927–1941*. Solomons: Calvert Marine Museum, 1986, 54 pp. Seized German vessels from World War I that were "mothballed" south of Point Patience.

————. *"Solomons Mines": A History of the U. S. Naval Mine Warfare Test Station, Solomons, Maryland, 1942–1947*. Solomons: Calvert Marine Museum, 1987, 46 pp.

————. "Tankers in the Patuxent: The ESSO Fleet Lay–up Site in the 1930s." *The American Neptune*, Winter 1987, pp. 45-53.

Conant, Melvin A. *I Remember: Recollections of "Pepper" Langley Growing Up in Solomons*. Solomons: Privately Printed, 1990, 115 pp.

Footner, Geoffrey M. *The Last Generation: A History of a Chesapeake Shipbuilding Family*. Solomons: Calvert Marine Museum Press, 1991, 194 pp. Definitive information about the M. M. Davis & Son Shipyard, including much background on Solomons.

Footner, Hulbert. *Charles' Gift: Salute to a Maryland House of 1650*. New York: Harper & Brothers, 1939, 290 pp. Much of the information in this book relates to Mr. Footner's experiences as a newcomer to Solomons and Calvert County prior to World War II.

Hammett, Regina C. *History of St. Mary's County, Maryland, 1634–1990*. Rev. ed. Ridge: The Author, 1991, 631 pp.

Harrison, Edith Marsh. *Descendant of a Chesapeake Shipbuilder (A Family Genealogy)*. Baltimore: Privately Printed, 1992, 42 pp. Mrs. Harrison's forebears ran the J. T. Marsh Shipyard at Solomons.

Johnson, Paula J., ed. *Working the Water: The Commercial Fisheries of Maryland's Patuxent River*. Charlottesville: University Press of Virginia and Calvert Marine Museum, 1988, 218 pp. Articles on seafood industries, especially in the Patuxent area, as well as a catalogue of fisheries items in the collections of the Calvert Marine Museum.

Lankford, Irene Martin. *Our Lady Star of the Sea, 1888–1988*. Solomons: Privately Printed, 1988, 19 pp.

Lore, Joseph Cobb. "Some Reminiscences of Joseph C. Lore Jr. of Solomons Island, Maryland. *The Solomons Islander*, June 1989–July 1990.

Stein, Charles F. *A History of Calvert County, Maryland*. Prince Frederick: Calvert County Historical Society, 1976, 484 pp.

Tongue, Thomas O. *A History of Saint Peter's Chapel: Religious Activities in Lower Calvert County, Maryland Prior to 1889 and the Next 100 Years*. Solomons: Privately Printed, 1989, 30 pp.

Related Works

Brewington, Marion Vernon. *Chesapeake Bay Log Canoes and Bugeyes*. Cambridge: Cornell Maritime Press, 1963, 171 pp. Boatbuilders and bugeyes from Solomons are described.

Burgess, Robert H., and H. Graham Wood. *Steamboats Out of Baltimore*. Cambridge: Tidewater Publishers, 1968, 236 pp. Steamboats serving Solomons and the Patuxent are included.

Footner, Hulbert. *Maryland Main and the Eastern Shore*. New York: D. Appleton–Century Company, 1942, 331 pp.

————. *Sailor of Fortune: The Life and Adventures of Commodore Barney, U.S.N.* New York: Harper & Brothers, 1940, 323 pp. Special emphasis on the War of 1812 in the Patuxent.

Gillespie, C. Richard. *The James Adams Floating Theatre*. Centreville, MD: Tidewater Publishers, 1991, 288 pp. Visits to Solomons and the Patuxent are included.

Holly, David C. *Tidewater by Steamboat: A Saga of the Chesapeake. The Weems Line on the Patuxent, Potomac, and Rappahannock*. Baltimore: Johns Hopkins University Press in cooperation with the Calvert Marine Museum, 1991, 314 pp. This was the principal line serving Solomons and the Patuxent.

Powledge, Fred. *Working River*. New York: Farrar, Straus and Giroux, 1995, 136 pp. The river depicted is the Patuxent.

Sherwood, Donald H. *The Sailing Years*. [no place]: The Author, 1971, 91 pp. Mr. Sherwood's first yacht was built at Solomons.

Shomette, Donald G. *Flotilla: Battle for the Patuxent*. Solomons: Calvert Marine Museum Press, 1981, 247 pp. Action on the Patuxent during the War of 1812.

————. *The Othello Affair: The Pursuit of French Pirates on Patuxent River, Maryland, August 1807*. Solomons: Calvert Marine Museum Press, 1985, 37 pp.

————. *Tidewater Time Capsule: History Beneath the Patuxent*. Centreville, MD: Tidewater Publishers, 1995, 370 pp.

Tilp, Frederick. *The Chesapeake Bay of Yore: Mainly About the Rowing and Sailing Craft*. Alexandria: The Author, 1982, 148 pp.

Fictional Works

Brooks, Kenneth F. *Run to the Lee*. New York: W. W. Norton, 1965, 185 pp. Exciting events on a schooner in the Chesapeake Bay near Solomons.

Footner, Hulbert. *Cap'n Sue*. Garden City, NY: Doubleday, Doran & Co., 1927, 314 pp. A woman captain's adventures, largely on the Patuxent. Such a woman captain did exist.

————. *Country Love: A Stage Girl's Struggle Against Fame and Fortune*. London: Hodder and Stoughton, Ltd., 1920, 319 pp.

————. *The Dark Ships*. New York: Harper, 1937, 284 pp. Mystery. Locale is Solomons in Calvert County, involving the mothballed German vessels.

————. *More than Bread*. Philadelphia: Lippincott, 1938, 365 pp. Story laid in Calvert County, with anecdotes involving Solomons.

————. *Ramshackle House*. New York: George H. Doran Co., 1922, 310 pp. Adventure story laid in Calvert County, at the Barreda mansion on Drum Point.

Mears, Richard C. *Ebb of the River: A Fictional Memoir*. New York: Wyndham Books, 1980, 205 pp. A boy's adventures in Solomons and on the Patuxent.

Salamanca, Jack Richard. *Embarkation*. New York: Alfred A. Knopf, 1973, 274 pp. Shipbuilding along the Calvert County shore, with references to Solomons.

————. *Southern Light*. New York: Alfred A. Knopf, 1986, 675 pp. Solomons is the locale of this novel.

INDEX BY SITE NUMBER